DAVID BEZ AKA SALADPRIDE AKA THE PRIDEKITCHEN

VEGANLOVE

CREATE QUICK, EASY, EVERYDAY MEALS WITH
A VEG + A PROTEIN + A SAUCE + A TOPPING.

K

An Hachette UK Company
www.hachette.co.uk

First published in Great Britain in 2022 by Kyle Books,
an imprint of Octopus Publishing Group Limited
Carmelite House
50 Victoria Embankment
London EC4Y 0DZ

ISBN: 978 1 91423 916 8

Publishing Director: Judith Hannam
Publisher: Joanna Copestick
Copy-editor: Vicki Murrell
Editorial Assistant: Zakkaria Raja
Design and photography: David Bez
Production: Katherine Hockley

A Cataloguing in Publication record for this title is available from the British Library.

Printed and bound in Italy.

10 9 8 7 6 5 4 3 2 1

CONTENTS

WHY VEGAN?

I grew up eating well from when I was very little – I come from Milan, Italy, and both my mom and my dad were really great cooks. Although I've never been a foodie, and haven't ever been interested in fancy restaurants, I guess you could say that I have a good knowledge about delicious food.

As far as my food career is concerned, everything started a few years ago when I came to London to work as an art director in the TV and graphic design industry. I stumbled across the fact that nutrition has a very important role in health. So, I started a blog called Salad Pride by taking daily pictures of my lunch in the office. I made one new recipe a day from my desk for three years. My blog became globally successful and it transformed into my debut book, *SaladLove*. The press called me 'the man who sexed up salad', which was ironic, as I hated salads when I was young and was not really into veggies when I was in Italy. I was the classic Italian man who loves pasta!

SaladLove was published in 2014 and was followed by *BreakfastLove* and *SupperLove*. Back in 2016, while writing *SupperLove*, I began to feel increasingly reluctant to both cook and eat meat – in fact I felt pretty sick about it – and came to realize that it was my body protesting and simply refusing to do it any longer.

At the time, I had a café, called SaladPride, in Covent Garden, London, so I decided to make it entirely vegan. Although it's become increasingly fashionable recently to go vegan, for me it was a real calling and a response to the path my body was telling me to take. Initially, I was drawn more towards simply increasing the amount of fruit and veggies I ate, but slowly, as my awareness of the issues surrounding animal welfare and the consequences of animal farming on the planet grew, I decided I no longer wanted to eat meat at all.

All around the world, supermarket shelves have been filled with vegan products designed to offer the consumer direct replacements for the meat and cheese with which they are familiar. Many of these products are highly processed, unnatural and not very healthy (plus most of the time they don't even taste very nice).

While I know that many people derive comfort from eating something that resembles their previous diet, I know, too, that a lot of vegans (and also non-vegans, for that matter) would like to be more mindful with their choices, and to be able to enjoy good food, not overly processed mockery. And when you start to explore the wealth of natural foods that are available, you see just how much there is to discover and enjoy.

ABOUT THIS BOOK

The reason I've written this book is not to 'veganize' traditional meat recipes, but to create new, plant-based classics, and to bring big veggies to the next level and show how simple and tasty they can be.

Although all the ingredients in the recipes can be bought in supermarkets, where you buy your produce from can have a significant impact, so I would urge you, if possible, to source your veggies from local markets or to subscribe to a local organic box scheme. This may mean you are confronted with veggies that you've previously avoided, thinking: 'What can I do with that big root?!' or 'I don't even know what that tastes like.' That was my reaction when I received my first organic box and found, along with the expected potatoes, tomatoes and cucumbers, a lot of unknown (to me) veggies, such as swedes, turnips, parsnips and so on!

Like my three previous books, this one is an exploration. I'm not here to tell you how to cook or to teach you some fancy technique, because I'm not chef.

I am just a curious person who wants to find solutions to simple problems – in this case, how to elevate veggies into the kind of meals that satisfy even non-vegans. To simplify my exploration, I gave myself rules and set some boundaries, with the result that every meal consists of the same four components:

1. ONE BIG, DOMINANT VEGGIE (THE MAIN)
2. ONE CARB OR PROTEIN SIDE (PULSES, STARCHES OR GRAINS)
3. ONE SAUCE OR CREAM OR DRESSING
4. ONE OR TWO TOPPINGS (HERBS & CRUNCH)

COOKING BIG VEGGIES

To create the mains, I've selected a range of day-to-day veggies, but also some more unusual ones. Some of them are very common and can be found everywhere, in every country in the world. Others may be more specific to the Northern hemisphere. I decided to treat these big veggies as you would meat or fish, so I've slow-cooked them, roasted them, pan-fried them, grilled (broiled) them and, of course, marinated them; adding spices and flavour. I tried cutting the veggies into different sizes, cooking them whole, but also halving them and even making them into 'steaks' and layering them. I also grouped them into types:

CELERIAC (CELERY ROOT), SWEET POTATO, BEETROOT (BEET), ONION, TURNIP, SWEDE, CARROT, PARSNIP

Root vegetables can be hard to make interesting because they are very dense, and flavour often struggles to find a way through. However, by applying different cooking techniques, it is possible to create meals that are both satisfying and delicious. You can, for example, marinate them overnight with salt, which also ferments them, or with acids, such as lemon, that 'cook' them a bit.

Scoring root veggies helps aid the cooking process and encourages the flavourings to penetrate. If you want to speed up the cooking process, you can cover the veggies and steam them for half their cooking time. I tend to begin by searing them, as you would do a piece of meat, which creates a layer of flavour as it caramelizes the external layer of the veg.

Then, I usually roast them in the oven, basting them with their marinade to protect them. I do the same when cooking them in a pan or skillet – never let your veggies dry out.

CAULIFLOWER, FENNEL, CABBAGE, SQUASH

These big, fibrous veggies often require longer cooking, and need to be treated in a similar way to root veggies.

COURGETTE (ZUCCHINI), MUSHROOM, BROCCOLI, AUBERGINE (EGGPLANT), (BELL) PEPPER

These veggies require much less time and effort, and a different type of cooking applies to them. In fact, some of them need very little cooking at all. Broccoli, for example, can be treated very similarly to cauliflower, but requires much less cooking time (the florets can burn quite easily).

Courgettes also need very little cooking as, if you cook for too long, they start releasing a lot of water. You want, therefore, to catch them when they are still slightly firm and have a good bite.

With mushrooms, it really depends on their type, so I have given specific instructions in each recipe.

LETTUCE, RADICCHIO, TOMATO

In the summer, it's good to have recipes for more salad-y type veggies. Salad leaves and tomatoes can obviously be eaten raw, but they can also be charred briefly on a high heat, which gives them a delicious flavour, but again you don't want to cook them too much.

MARINADES

Marinades help tenderize and impart incredible flavour into your big veggies, particularly if they are left to infuse overnight, though even 30 minutes will make a difference.

Basic marinades are made with three main elements:

1. an acid, such as vinegar, lemon juice, beer or wine, which will pre-'cook' the veg.
2. oil, spices and seasoning, which can include garlic, ginger, fresh herbs and spices.
3. salt, to break down the fibres and make the veggies release some of their liquid.

Don't discard the marinade once you've removed the veg. It can be used to baste the veg when roasting it, to keep it moist, but also later on, when you're creating gravies or flavouring sauces.

PULSES, STARCHES & GLUTEN-FREE GRAINS

Each one of my veggies is paired with a comforting and filling pulse, starch or grain.

Pulses are low fat, as well as being excellent sources of fibre and protein, plus they are full of vitamins and minerals. They are also good for the planet, as they have a low carbon footprint and enrich the soil, so are sustainable as well as healthy. If you want to eat pulses in their optimal state, it is best to buy dried versions, which will need to be soaked overnight and then cooked, or to sprout them yourself. It's also much more economical to do this.

If you're really busy, canned versions are more convenient, though they are often unseasoned and pretty bland. Jarred pulses are usually better quality. I've created some nifty tricks to add more flavour to them by adding spices, fresh herbs and sometimes veggies (such as onions, carrots, tomatoes, spinach and so on), which also enriches them with nutrients.

All the starches and grains I use are gluten-free. Although I'm not coeliac, like many others I am sensitive to gluten and find it adversely affects my digestion (in the form of air mostly!). Along with rice, I've also used less common grains, such as quinoa, buckwheat and oats and also starches, such as corn and potatoes, as they are both very filling and complement the big veggies well.

SAUCES

To bind together the main veg and the pulses, grains and starches, I have come up with a series of easy-to-make sauces. These add creaminess and flavour to the dishes. I've made them super-easy, but if you are pushed for time, you might sometimes want to use off-the-shelf ones (there are hundreds available at the supermarket).

There are two main types of sauces:

1. cooked sauces, such as tomato, béchamel, gravy and curry. These often require a bit of effort.
2. raw sauces, such as pestos, guacamole and nut creams. These are usually created by blending or mixing ingredients and do not require any cooking at all.

TOPPINGS & HERBS

These little touches will lift your dishes to another level and ensure they taste incredible.

Toppings are small flavour bombs that add texture and crunch, saltiness or sweetness. They include nuts, seeds, coconut flakes, dried fruit, capers, olives, pickles and sauerkraut; all of which can easily be found on supermarket shelves.

I don't usually recommend adding dried spices at this stage as they tend to overpower a dish, though a sprinkle of chilli pepper flakes, smoked paprika or a grinding of black pepper can be very good.

For the final touch, to add freshness and even more flavour, I always have fresh herbs to hand (usually on my window ledge). I can't imagine doing without basil, mint, oregano, tarragon, coriander (cilantro) and so on!

Enjoy. And buon appetito!

RECIPES

ALTERNATIVE TIP

Swap the cream for the hot and spicy Tomato Sauce on page 180.

STUFFED RED (BELL) PEPPER WITH ALMOND CREAM

INGREDIENTS

PROTEIN/CARB
50g (2oz) cooked white rice
1 tablespoon olive oil
1 teaspoon sea salt

MAIN VEG
1 large red (bell) pepper
1 tablespoon olive oil
a sprinkle of sea salt

SAUCE
1 tablespoon capers
1 tablespoon olive oil
1 tablespoon chopped fresh mint
½ teaspoon sea salt
100ml (3½fl oz) single (light) cream
 (almond, oat or soy)

TOPPING
a handful of black olives, pitted
¾ sun-dried tomato in oil
1 spring onion (scallion), finely chopped
1 tablespoon capers
a sprinkle of finely chopped fresh mint

METHOD

PROTEIN/CARB
In a bowl, mix the cooked rice with the oil and half the topping ingredients and season with the salt.

MAIN VEG
Preheat the oven to 200°C (400°F)/gas mark 6. Slice off the top of the pepper and remove the seeds. Place the pepper on a baking tray (sheet) lined with baking paper, drizzle with olive oil and sprinkle with salt. Bake for 25–30 minutes, depending on size, until the pepper is softer, but still slightly firm. Fill with the cooked rice and return to the oven to toast for a few minutes.

SAUCE
In a bowl, crush the capers together with the oil, mint and salt, then stir in the cream.

ASSEMBLING
Place the stuffed pepper on a plate, drizzle with the sauce and scatter over the remaining black olives, sun-dried tomato, spring onion, capers and a sprinkle of fresh mint.

 WATCH
THE ONLINE
RECIPE

ROASTED (BELL) PEPPER WITH BROAD (FAVA) BEANS & HUMMUS

INGREDIENTS

PROTEIN/CARB
50g (2oz) fresh broad (fava) beans

MAIN VEG
1 green (bell) pepper
1 tablespoon olive oil
a pinch of sea salt

SAUCE
2 tablespoons chickpea hummus
1 tablespoon extra virgin olive oil
1 teaspoon lemon juice

TOPPING
a handful of goji berries, soaked in
  a little warm water
a sprinkle of hemp seeds
a sprinkle of finely chopped fresh parsley

METHOD

PROTEIN/CARB
Remove the beans from their pods and then remove the skin. They will naturally split in half. You can eat them raw, as they are, or you can steam them for a minute or two.

MAIN VEG
Preheat the oven to 200°C (400°F)/gas mark 6. Slice off the top of the pepper and remove the seeds. Place the pepper on a baking tray (sheet) lined with baking paper, drizzle with olive oil and sprinkle with salt. Bake for 25–30 minutes, depending on size, until the pepper is softer, but still slightly firm. If you prefer, you can remove the skin at this point, although I like to keep it.

SAUCE
Place the hummus in a bowl and stir in the extra virgin olive oil and lemon juice to make it runnier.

ASSEMBLING
Spoon the sauce onto a plate and lay the roasted pepper on top. Scatter over the beans, along with the goji berries, hemp seeds and a sprinkle of fresh parsley.

ALTERNATIVE TIP
If you struggle to find fresh
broad beans, you can use
frozen ones or edamame (just
defrost them and they will
work perfectly). You can also
use canned cannellini beans.

ALTERNATIVE TIP
If you like Mexican-style chilli beans, why not mix them in the hot and spicy Tomato Sauce on page 180?

YELLOW (BELL) PEPPER WITH BLACK CHICKPEAS (GARBANZO BEANS) & CORIANDER (CILANTRO) PESTO

INGREDIENTS

PROTEIN/CARB
120g (4¼oz) black chickpeas
   (garbanzo beans), cooked
1 tablespoon olive oil
a pinch of sea salt

MAIN VEG
1 yellow (bell) pepper
1 tablespoon olive oil
a pinch of sea salt

SAUCE
a bunch of fresh coriander (cilantro)
3 tablespoons olive oil
a pinch of sea salt
1 teaspoon lemon juice
1 teaspoon broken cashew nuts

TOPPING
a sprinkle of broken cashew nuts
a sprinkle of fresh coriander (cilantro)

METHOD

PROTEIN/CARB
Place the cooked chickpeas in a bowl and stir through the olive oil and add a pinch of salt.

MAIN VEG
Preheat the oven to 200°C (400°F)/gas mark 6. Slice off the top of the pepper and remove the seeds. Place the pepper on a baking tray (sheet) lined with baking paper, drizzle with olive oil and sprinkle with salt. Bake for 25–30 minutes, depending on size, until the pepper is softer, but still slightly firm.

SAUCE
Place the coriander, olive oil, salt and lemon juice in a blender and blend until smooth, then add the cashews and stir. Spoon the sauce onto a plate but save 2 tablespoons for the filling.

ASSEMBLING
Add the reserved sauce to the chickpea mixture and then spoon this into the pepper. Arrange the pepper on top of the sauce on the plate and scatter over a handful of cashews and a sprinkle of fresh coriander (cilantro).

RED (BELL) PEPPER WITH COCONUT YOGURT & SMOKED PAPRIKA LENTILS

INGREDIENTS

PROTEIN/CARB
60g (2¹⁄₂oz) brown lentils
1 teaspoon vegetable stock (broth)
1 teaspoon coconut or brown sugar
1 teaspoon smoked paprika
¹⁄₂ teaspoon cayenne pepper
1 tablespoon lemon juice
2 tablespoons olive oil
¹⁄₂ teaspoon sea salt

MAIN VEG
1 large red (bell) pepper
1 tablespoon olive oil
a pinch of sea salt

SAUCE
2 tablespoons vegan (coconut, soy
   or oat) yogurt

TOPPING
a sprinkle of raisins
a sprinkle of fresh thyme

METHOD

PROTEIN/CARB
Rinse the lentils with fresh water before cooking to remove any dust or debris. Transfer to a pan, cover with 180ml (6¹⁄₄fl oz) water and bring to the boil. Add the vegan stock (broth), sugar, smoked paprika, cayenne pepper and lemon juice, mix well and cover tightly. Reduce the heat and simmer until the lentils are tender (15–20 minutes). Stir through the oil and salt after cooking.

MAIN VEG
Preheat the oven to 200°C (400°F)/gas mark 6. Slice off the top of the pepper and remove the seeds. Place the pepper on a baking tray (sheet) lined with baking paper, drizzle with olive oil and sprinkle with salt. Bake for 25–30 minutes, depending on size, until the pepper is softer, but still slightly firm.

SAUCE
Fill the pepper with 1 teaspoon of cooked lentils and the vegan yogurt.

ASSEMBLING
Spread the remaining lentils out over a plate and top with the filled pepper. Scatter over the raisins and fresh thyme and serve.

WATCH
THE ONLINE
RECIPE

ALTERNATIVE TIP

Why not try the spicy tomato sauce on page 180, if you like Mexican-style chilli beans?

ALTERNATIVE TIP
If you like a creamier sauce,
replace half the oil with half
an avocado.

GREEN (BELL) PEPPER WITH CHIMICHURRI

INGREDIENTS

PROTEIN/CARB

80g (2¾ oz) gluten-free bread,
  broken into 2.5cm (1in) chunks
1 tablespoon olive oil
a sprinkle of sea salt

MAIN VEG

1 large green (bell) pepper
1 tablespoon olive oil
a pinch of sea salt

SAUCE

2 tablespoons roughly chopped
  fresh garlic
8 tablespoons finely chopped
  fresh parsley
8 tablespoons finely chopped
  fresh coriander (cilantro)
4 tablespoons fresh
  lemon juice
½ fresh red chilli pepper,
  finely chopped
225ml (8 fl oz) olive oil
½ tablespoon sea salt, plus more
  to taste

TOPPING

½ fresh red chilli pepper,
  finely chopped
a handful of finely chopped fresh
  flat-leaf parsley

METHOD

PROTEIN/CARB

Preheat the oven to 200°C (400°F)/gas mark 6. Arrange the gluten-free bread on a baking tray (sheet) lined with baking paper, drizzle with olive oil, sprinkle with salt and toast for only a few minutes until crispy on the outside but still soft on the inside.

MAIN VEG

Preheat the oven to 200°C (400°F)/gas mark 6. Slice off the top of the pepper and remove the seeds. Place the pepper on a baking tray (sheet) lined with baking paper, drizzle with olive oil and sprinkle with salt. Bake for 25–30 minutes, depending on size, until the pepper is softer, but still slightly firm.

SAUCE

Place the garlic in a food processor and pulse until minced, then add the parsley, coriander (cilantro) and lemon juice and process until well combined. Finally add the chilli, oil and salt and pulse again until well combined. Check for seasoning again and add more salt if necessary.

ASSEMBLING

Mix the toasted bread with the sauce and fill the pepper. Spoon the remaining bread and sauce mix onto the middle of a plate, arrange the pepper on top and scatter over the chilli and parsley.

ROASTED RED (BELL) PEPPER WITH POTATO & CURRY SAUCE

INGREDIENTS

PROTEIN/CARB
1 large potato, peeled and chopped
  into 2.5cm (1in) cubes

MAIN VEG
1 red (bell) pepper
1 tablespoon olive oil
a pinch of sea salt

SAUCE
200ml (7fl oz) coconut milk
1 teaspoon miso paste
1 teaspoon ground cumin
1 teaspoon ground ginger
1 teaspoon ground turmeric
1 teaspoon salt
1 teaspoon chilli flakes or 1 small
  fresh chilli, finely chopped
a handful of fresh coriander (cilantro)
  stalks
zest and juice of ½ lime

TOPPING
1 tablespoon raisins
1 tablespoon toasted coconut flakes
a sprinkle of chopped fresh coriander
  (cilantro)

METHOD

PROTEIN/CARB
Steam the potato for 15 minutes until soft but not crumbly.

MAIN VEG
Preheat the oven to 200°C (400°F)/gas mark 6. Slice off the top of the pepper and remove the seeds. Place the pepper on a baking tray (sheet) lined with baking paper, drizzle with olive oil and sprinkle with salt. Bake for 25–30 minutes, depending on size, until the pepper is softer, but still slightly firm. If you prefer, you can remove the skin at this point, although I like to keep it.

SAUCE
Place all the ingredients in a blender and blend until smooth, then pour into a pan over a low heat to warm through (do not boil).

ASSEMBLING
Stir the potato into the sauce, then spoon into a shallow bowl. Arrange the pepper on top and scatter over the raisins, coconut flakes and fresh coriander (cilantro).

ALTERNATIVE TIP
How about swapping the
curry sauce for the awesome
Italian tomato sauce on
page 67, and swap the
toppings for parsley and
black olives?

ALTERNATIVE TIP
This recipe works well with many different fillings, like other beans, chickpeas, buckwheat, rice, breadcrumbs and so on.

STUFFED TOMATO WITH AVOCADO CREAM & BLACK BEANS

INGREDIENTS

PROTEIN/CARB

1 tablespoon extra virgin olive oil

1 small shallot, finely chopped

120g (4¼oz) cooked black beans

½ teaspoon sea salt

sea salt and freshly ground black pepper, to taste

MAIN VEG

1 big beefy tomato

1 teaspoon extra virgin olive oil

SAUCE

3 tablespoons guacamole

1 teaspoon lemon juice

1 teaspoon extra virgin olive oil

TOPPING

a sprinkle of chilli flakes

a sprinkle of chopped fresh coriander (cilantro)

METHOD

PROTEIN/CARB

Heat the olive oil in a pan over a medium heat and cook the shallot until transparent but not burned, then add the beans and salt. Stir well and heat through, then season to taste.

MAIN VEG

Slice the top off the tomato and scoop out the pulp and seeds from the core, then fill it with the bean mixture. I prefer not to cook the stuffed tomato as I like the freshness and firmness of it raw, but you can also char it slightly on a very hot pan for few minutes.

SAUCE

Place all the ingredients in a blender and blend until smooth and creamy.

ASSEMBLING

Spread the sauce over a plate, arrange the stuffed tomato on top and then scatter over the chilli flakes and coriander (cilantro).

TOMATO STEAK ON CHICKPEA (GARBANZO BEAN) PANCAKE WITH HUMMUS

INGREDIENTS

PROTEIN/CARB

50g (2oz) chickpea (garbanzo bean) flour
2 tablespoons potato or corn starch
1 tablespoon + 1 teaspoon extra
   virgin olive oil
2 teaspoons salt
a handful of fresh oregano leaves

MAIN VEG

1 big beefy tomato
sea salt and freshly ground black pepper,
   to taste

SAUCE

120g (4¼oz) cooked chickpeas
2 tablespoons olive oil
1 teaspoon lemon juice
¼ teaspoon salt

TOPPING

a handful of fresh oregano
a sprinkle of pine nuts, toasted if liked
a drizzle of balsamic glaze

METHOD

PROTEIN/CARB

Tip the flour and starch into a bowl or blender. Slowly pour in 1 tablespoon oil (reserving the rest for later) and 150ml (5fl oz) water, beating with a whisk until you have a smooth, light batter (no lumps). Sprinkle over the salt and oregano and mix well.

Heat the remaining teaspoon of oil in a non-stick frying pan over a medium–high heat. Pour in the batter, tilting the pan a little to ensure a thin and even layer. When the sides are crispy enough and the top is bubbly, use a spatula to gently flip the pancake and cook the other side. Keep flipping until you reach your preferred consistency – I like it pretty crispy, so I cook it for a bit longer.

MAIN VEG

Slice the top off the tomato, making sure the hard bit is removed, then slice horizontally into 1cm- (⅓in-) thick layers (steaks). Season and set aside.

SAUCE

Place all the ingredients in a blender with 1 tablespoon water and blend until smooth.

ASSEMBLING

Spoon the sauce onto a plate, then layer with the pancake and finally the sliced tomato steaks. Scatter over the oregano and pine nuts and finish with a drizzle of balsamic glaze.

ALTERNATIVE TIP
This recipe also works well
with the basil pesto on
page 39, the creamy vegan
'ricotta', also on page 39, or
caper yogurt on page 36.

ALTERNATIVE TIP
You can jazz this recipe up by
adding 1 more teaspoon of
mustard to the sauce or make
it healthier by using a vegan
yogurt instead of the mayo.
Also, a basil pesto would
make a great sauce.

STUFFED TOMATO WITH MAYO & STEAMED POTATO

INGREDIENTS

PROTEIN/CARB
1 large potato, peeled and chopped
   into 2.5cm (1in) cubes

MAIN VEG
1 big beefy tomato
1 tablespoon olive oil
a pinch of sea salt

SAUCE
3 tablespoons vegan mayo
1 tablespoon vegan milk (oat or rice)
1 teaspoon English mustard
sea salt and freshly ground
   black pepper, to taste

TOPPING
a handful of fresh chives, finely chopped
a sprinkle of smoked paprika
plenty of sea salt and freshly ground
   black pepper, to taste

METHOD

PROTEIN/CARB
Steam the potato for 15 minutes until soft but not crumbly.

MAIN VEG
Slice the top off the tomato and scoop out the pulp and seeds from the core.

SAUCE
Place all the ingredients in a bowl, mix well and set aside.

ASSEMBLING
Mix the potato into the sauce and then fill the tomato with the mix. I prefer not to cook the stuffed tomato as I like the freshness and firmness of the raw tomato, but you can also burn it slightly on a very hot pan for few minutes.

Spoon the remaining mixture onto a plate, arrange the stuffed tomato on top, sprinkle over the chives and smoked paprika and season well.

CORN-STUFFED TOMATO WITH CAPERS & YOGURT

INGREDIENTS

PROTEIN/CARB

1 tablespoon extra virgin olive oil
1 small shallot, finely chopped
120g (4¼oz) sweetcorn
  (canned or frozen)
½ teaspoon sea salt
sea salt and freshly ground black
  pepper, to taste

MAIN VEG

1 big beefy tomato

SAUCE

3 tablespoons vegan yogurt (coconut
  is my fave)
1 teaspoon extra virgin olive oil
1 teaspoon lemon juice
1 teaspoon capers
sea salt and freshly ground
  black pepper, to taste

TOPPING

1 teaspoon capers
a sprinkle of fresh oregano leaves

METHOD

PROTEIN/CARB

Heat the olive oil in a pan over a medium heat and cook the shallot until transparent but not burned, then add the corn and salt. Stir well and heat through, then season to taste.

MAIN VEG

Slice the tomato in half horizontally and scoop out the pulp and seeds from the core, then fill it with the cooked corn. I prefer not to cook the stuffed tomato as I like the freshness and firmness of it raw, but you can also char it slightly on a very hot pan for a few minutes.

SAUCE

Place all the ingredients in a bowl and mix well.

ASSEMBLING

Spoon the sauce onto a plate, arrange the stuffed tomato on top and scatter over the capers and fresh oregano.

ALTERNATIVE TIP
This recipe works well
with many different
fillings, like other beans,
chickpeas, buckwheat, rice,
breadcrumbs and so on. You
can also try it with other
sauces, like the pesto on page
39 or 148, the tahini sauce
on page 63, or the avocado
sauce on page 175.

ALTERNATIVE TIP
If you don't have the time
to make the 'ricotta', there
are plenty of soft vegan,
cheeze-like creams in the
supermarket.

SLICED TOMATO WITH BASIL PESTO & ALMOND 'RICOTTA'

INGREDIENTS

PROTEIN/CARB
100g (3½oz) blanched almonds
½ teaspoon sea salt
2 teaspoons lemon juice
sea salt and freshly ground black pepper,
  to taste

MAIN VEG
1 big beefy tomato
1 teaspoon extra virgin olive oil
sea salt and freshly ground
  black pepper, to taste

SAUCE
a bunch of fresh basil
3–4 tablespoons olive oil
1 teaspoon lemon juice
¼ teaspoon sea salt
1 teaspoon nutritional yeast
2 tablespoons almond flakes

TOPPING
a sprinkle of almond flakes
a handful of fresh basil leaves

METHOD

PROTEIN/CARB
Place the almonds and salt with 150ml (5fl oz) water in a high-speed blender and blitz to combine. Transfer to a small saucepan and bring to the boil, then turn off the heat and add the lemon juice, stirring gently for a few minutes. Drain the liquid through a classic cheesecloth or just a colander or sieve into a bowl, then leave the almond 'ricotta' in the fridge overnight to release the rest of the water. Taste and adjust the seasoning if necessary.

MAIN VEG
Slice the top off the tomato, making sure the hard bit is removed, then slice horizontally into 1cm (⅓in) layers. Season and set aside.

SAUCE
Place the basil, olive oil, lemon juice and salt with the nutritional yeast and half the almonds in a blender and blend until smooth, then stir through the remaining nuts.

ASSEMBLING
Layer the tomato on a plate and fill each layer with sauce and a little 'ricotta'. Spoon the remaining sauce, olive oil and 'ricotta' on top and sprinkle with almond flakes and fresh basil.

LETTUCE WITH GUACAMOLE & BLACK BEANS

INGREDIENTS

PROTEIN/CARB
120g (4¼oz) cooked black beans
1 tablespoon olive oil
a pinch of sea salt

MAIN VEG
½ cos (romaine) lettuce head, halved
1 teaspoon extra virgin olive oil

SAUCE
1 fresh green chilli, finely chopped
½ spring onion (scallion), thinly sliced
1 ripe avocado
¼ grapefruit, juice of
sea salt, to taste

TOPPING
a sprinkle of toasted almond flakes
a sprinkle of fresh dill
1 tablespoon roughly chopped pink
  grapefruit segments

METHOD

PROTEIN/CARB
In a bowl, mix the black beans with oil and salt and set aside.

MAIN VEG
Place a pan over a high heat and, using tongs, lay the lettuce, cut-side down, to char slightly for 2–3 minutes, adding the oil at the end.

SAUCE
Place all the ingredients in a blender and blend until smooth.

ASSEMBLING
Spoon the sauce onto a plate, followed by the beans. Place the lettuce on top and scatter over the toppings.

ALTERNATIVE TIP
You can make a more classic guacamole by replacing the grapefruit with 1 teaspoon lime juice and 2 cherry tomatoes.

ALTERNATIVE TIP

If you don't want to use this
pesto, many other sauces also
make a great match, like the
sun-dried tomato pesto on
page 60, the mustard mayo
on page 48, or caper
yogurt on page 36.

LETTUCE WITH CANNELLINI BEANS & CORIANDER (CILANTRO) PESTO

INGREDIENTS

PROTEIN/CARB
120g (4¼oz) cooked cannellini beans
1 tablespoon olive oil
a pinch of sea salt

MAIN VEG
½ cos (romaine) lettuce head, halved
1 teaspoon extra virgin olive oil
sea salt and freshly ground
  black pepper, to taste

SAUCE
a bunch of fresh coriander (cilantro)
3–4 tablespoons olive oil
1 teaspoon lemon juice
¼ teaspoon sea salt
1 teaspoon nutritional yeast
2 tablespoons broken cashews

TOPPING
a sprinkle of broken cashews
a sprinkle of fresh coriander (cilantro)

METHOD

PROTEIN/CARB
In a bowl, mix the beans with the olive oil and salt and set aside.

MAIN VEG
Place a frying pan over a high heat and, using tongs, lay the lettuce in the hot pan, cut-side down, to char slightly for 2–3 minutes. Drizzle over the oil at the end and season with salt.

SAUCE
Place the coriander (cilantro), olive oil, lemon juice and salt with the nutritional yeast and half the cashews in a blender and blend until smooth, then stir through the remaining nuts.

ASSEMBLING
Drizzle 1 tablespoon of sauce on the plate and spoon the beans on. Arrange the lettuce on top and scatter over the cashews and coriander (cilantro) with the remainder of the sauce on top.

LETTUCE, KIMCHI & BUCKWHEAT

INGREDIENTS

PROTEIN/CARB
60g (2 ½ oz) buckwheat
1 tablespoon olive oil
a pinch of sea salt
1 tablespoon vegan kimchi juice

MAIN VEG
½ cos (romaine) lettuce head, halved
2 tablespoons vegan kimchi juice or
  sauerkraut sauce

SAUCE
A.
3 tablespoons vegan kimchi
or
B.
3 tablespoons classic sauerkraut
1 teaspoon minced ginger
1 garlic clove, minced
1 teaspoon cayenne pepper
1 tablespoon miso paste
sea salt, to taste

TOPPING
a sprinkle of sesame seeds
1 spring onion (scallion),
  finely chopped
1 tablespoon vegan kimchi

METHOD

PROTEIN/CARB
Place the buckwheat in a saucepan with 120ml (3 ¾ fl oz) water
and bring to the boil, then reduce to a simmer, cover and cook
until the water has evaporated completely. Strain the buckwheat
through a colander and rinse under hot water to remove the
starchy and foxy bits. Set aside to drain, then when it's dry,
transfer to a bowl and stir through the oil, salt and kimchi juice.

MAIN VEG
Place the lettuce halves, together with the kimchi juice or
sauerkraut sauce in a resealable bag and massage the leaves to
infuse them with flavour. Set aside to marinade for a few minutes.

SAUCE
A. Take the kimchi and squeeze it to release the juice, reserving
this for the buckwheat and marinade. Set the rest of the kimchi
aside to use as a topping.

B. If you don't have kimchi but can find sauerkraut, you can make
something similar. Take the sauerkraut and squeeze it to release
the juice. Place the ginger, garlic, cayenne pepper and miso paste
in a blender, together with the sauerkraut juice, and blend until
smooth. Mix the sauerkraut into this mixture. Squeeze out the
sauerkraut juices and add salt to taste.

ASSEMBLING
Spoon the buckwheat onto a plate and lay the lettuce on top.
Sprinkle over the sesame seeds and spring onion and put the
reserved kimchi or sauerkraut on top.

ALTERNATIVE TIP
This recipe works very well
not just with buckwheat, but
also with basmati rice, tofu or
even beans and lentils.

ALTERNATIVE TIP
This recipe works very well with the bulgogi sauce, but also with the hot sriracha mayo on page 204, the BBQ sauce on page 100, or even the teriyaki sauce on page 195.

FRIED LETTUCE WITH BLACK RICE & BULGOGI SAUCE

INGREDIENTS

PROTEIN/CARB
120g (4¼oz) cooked black rice
1 tablespoon olive oil
a pinch of sea salt

MAIN VEG
½ cos (romaine) lettuce head, halved
90g (3oz) buckwheat flour
30g (1oz) cornstarch
½ teaspoon sea salt
250ml (9fl oz) sparkling water
500ml (18fl oz) vegetable oil

SAUCE
½ pear, cored
½ garlic clove, chopped
1 tablespoon miso sauce
½ tablespoon grated fresh ginger
1 teaspoon roasted sesame oil
juice of ½ grapefruit

TOPPING
a sprinkle of sesame seeds
1 spring onion (scallion),
 finely chopped

RECIPE

PROTEIN/CARB
Heat the black rice and olive oil in a pan. Place in a bowl, salt and set aside (but keep it warm).

MAIN VEG
Place the lettuce halves with the sauce in a resealable bag and massage the leaves to infuse them with flavour. Set aside to marinade for a few minutes.

Next, make the batter: place the flour in a bowl with the salt and starch and whisk in the sparkling water. Dip the lettuce into the batter, to lightly coat, shaking off any excess.

Heat the oil in a large, shallow pan or wok and, when it's hot, fry the lettuce for 1–2 minutes, then flip over and cook for 1–2 minutes on the other side. You could also use a fryer, but I prefer this method.

SAUCE
Place all the ingredients in a blender and blend until smooth.

ASSEMBLING
Spoon the sauce onto a plate and top with the rice, then arrange the lettuce on top and sprinkle over sesame seeds and spring onion.

GRILLED LETTUCE, MUSTARD MAYO & CRISPY BUCKWHEAT CHUNKS

INGREDIENTS

PROTEIN/CARB

30g (1oz) buckwheat flour
½ tablespoon smoked paprika
125ml (4fl oz) plant-based milk
½ tablespoon tamari soy sauce
1 tablespoon vegetable oil

MAIN VEG

½ cos (romaine) lettuce head, halved
1 teaspoon extra virgin olive oil
sea salt, to taste

SAUCE

2 tablespoons vegan mayo
1 tablespoon vegan single (light)
  cream (oat)
1 teaspoon English mustard
1 tablespoon capers

TOPPING

½ spring onion (scallion),
  finely chopped
a sprinkle of chopped fresh
  flat-leaf parsley
2 sun-dried tomatoes, finely sliced

METHOD

PROTEIN/CARB

Tip the flour and paprika into a bowl and, beating with a whisk, pour in the milk and soy sauce until you have a smooth, light batter (no lumps). Heat the oil in a medium non-stick pan over a medium heat and pour in the batter, tilting the pan to ensure a thin and even layer. Cook for a minute, then stir the batter, as if you were making a scramble, until it firms up into crispy chunks. I like it pretty crispy, so I cook it for at least 10–15 minutes.

MAIN VEG

Place a frying pan over a high heat and, using tongs, lay the lettuce in the hot pan, cut-side down, to char slightly for 2–3 minutes. Drizzle over the oil at the end and season with salt.

SAUCE

Place all the ingredients in a blender and blend until smooth.

ASSEMBLING

Spoon the sauce onto one side of a plate and the crispy buckwheat on the other side. Arrange the lettuce on top with a final drizzle of sauce and scatter over the toppings.

ALTERNATIVE TIP
If you don't want to use the
buckwheat, you can use your
favourite gluten-free flour
mix or oat flour.

ALTERNATIVE TIP

If you don't have the chickpea (garbanzo bean) flour, you can use red lentil flour, yellow pea flour or even buckwheat flour.

COURGETTE (ZUCCHINI) WITH CRISPY CHICKPEA (GARBANZO BEAN) SCRAMBLE & DILL PESTO

INGREDIENTS

PROTEIN/CARB
50g (2oz) chickpea (garbanzo bean) flour
2 tablespoon extra virgin olive oil
1 tablespoon potato or cornstarch
1 teaspoon salt

MAIN VEG
1 courgette (zucchini)
1 tablespoon olive oil
a pinch of sea salt

SAUCE
3 tablespoons pumpkin seeds
2 garlic cloves, peeled
a large handful of roughly
  chopped fresh dill
zest of ½ lemon
1 teaspoon sea salt
125ml (4fl oz) olive oil

TOPPING
a handful of chopped fresh dill
a sprinkle of pumpkin seeds

METHOD

PROTEIN/CARB
Tip the flour and starch into a bowl or blender. Slowly pour in half the oil and 150ml (5fl oz) water, beating with a whisk until you have a smooth, light batter (no lumps). Season with the salt.

Heat the remaining oil in a non-stick frying pan over a medium–high heat. Pour in the batter, tilting the pan a little to ensure a thin and even layer. Cook for a minute, then stir the batter, as if you were making a scramble, until it firms up into crispy chunks. I like it pretty crispy, so I cook it for at least 10–15 minutes.

MAIN VEG
Pierce the courgette all over with a fork, then place in a hot pan (or griddle) set over a high heat. Keep turning it and squashing it for 15 minutes, so all the liquid comes out and it feels soft. Remove from the pan and set aside to cool a bit, then drizzle with oil and season with salt.

SAUCE
Place all the ingredients in a blender and blend until smooth.

ASSEMBLING
Spoon the sauce onto a plate, followed by the crispy chickpea scramble. To serve, arrange the courgette on top and scatter over the chopped fresh dill and pumpkin seeds.

COURGETTE (ZUCCHINI), RED QUINOA, PARSLEY & MINT SAUCE

INGREDIENTS

PROTEIN/CARB

50g (2oz) red quinoa

MAIN VEG

1 courgette (zucchini), halved
1 tablespoon olive oil
a pinch of sea salt

SAUCE

3 tablespoons shelled pistachios
a large sprig of fresh mint,
  roughly chopped
a large sprig of fresh flat-leaf parsley,
  roughly chopped
½ teaspoon sea salt
juice of ½ lemon
125ml (4fl oz) olive oil

TOPPING

a handful of fresh mint leaves
a handful of broken pistachios

METHOD

PROTEIN/CARB

Place the quinoa in a sieve and rinse under cold running water to remove all the soapy coating and get rid of any bitter flavour. Transfer the quinoa to a saucepan, cover with 100ml (3½fl oz) water and bring to the boil. Reduce the heat, cover with a lid and simmer for 15–20 minutes.

MAIN VEG

Place the courgette in a hot pan (or griddle) set over a high heat. Keep turning it and squashing it for 15 minutes, so all the liquid comes out and it feels soft. Remove from the pan and set aside to cool a bit, then drizzle with oil and season with salt.

SAUCE

Place all the ingredients in a blender and blend until smooth.

ASSEMBLING

Spoon the sauce onto a plate, followed by the quinoa and arrange the courgette on top. Finally, scatter over the toppings.

 WATCH
THE ONLINE
RECIPE

ALTERNATIVE TIP
This recipe works with any
type of protein or carb – you
can use beans, lentils, rice,
potato or buckwheat.

ALTERNATIVE TIP
If you want to make this
recipe lighter and fresher,
replace the tahini sauce with
the guacamole on page 40.

COURGETTE (ZUCCHINI) WITH BLACK BEANS & TAHINI

INGREDIENTS

PROTEIN/CARB
1 tablespoon olive oil
1 small onion, sliced
200g (7oz) black beans, drained
½ teaspoon brown sugar
sea salt, to taste

MAIN VEG
1 large courgette (zucchini)
extra virgin olive oil for brushing
sea salt and freshly ground black
  pepper, to taste

SAUCE
1 tablespoon tahini
3½ tablespoons plant-based milk
  (rice or oat work best)
1 teaspoon lemon juice
sea salt, to taste

TOPPING
extra virgin olive oil, for drizzling
a sprinkle of fresh thyme leaves
a pinch of paprika
1 teaspoon sesame seeds

METHOD

PROTEIN/CARB
Heat the olive oil in a pan over a medium heat and cook the sliced pieces of onion until transparent but not burned, then add the beans, sugar and salt. Stir well and heat through.

MAIN VEG
Using a sharp knife, score the courgette lengthways – each slice should cut about three-quarters of the way through and be spaced about 5mm (¼in) apart. Brush the courgette with olive oil, ensuring it gets down into all the slits, and season with salt and pepper.

Preheat the grill (broiler) to medium high. Place the sauce in a heatproof dish, arrange the courgette on top and grill (broil) for 30–35 minutes until the courgette is starting to soften but is still firm.

SAUCE
Place all the ingredients in a blender and blend until smooth. Check the consistency – add a little more tahini until creamy enough for you.

ASSEMBLING
Arrange the courgette and beans on a plate, pour over the sauce, drizzle with a little extra virgin olive oil and top with the toppings.

COURGETTE (ZUCCHINI) WITH TOMATO SAUCE & BREADCRUMBS

INGREDIENTS

PROTEIN/CARB

2 garlic cloves, finely chopped
80g (2¾oz) gluten-free breadcrumbs
a sprig of fresh rosemary

MAIN VEG

1 large courgette (zucchini)
extra virgin olive oil fir brushing
sea salt and freshly ground black pepper
   to taste

SAUCE

200ml (7fl oz) canned chopped tomatoes
1 teaspoon brown sugar
sea salt and freshly ground black pepper
   to taste

TOPPING

100ml (3½fl oz) single (light) cream
   (oat or rice)
a sprig of fresh rosemary
extra virgin olive oil, for drizzling

METHOD

PROTEIN/CARB

Preheat the oven to 200°C (400°F)/gas mark 6 for 10 minutes. Mix together the garlic, breadcrumbs and rosemary, then place in a roasting tin.

MAIN VEG

First make the sauce (see below). Using a sharp knife, score the courgette widthways – each slice should cut about three-quarters of the way through and be spaced about 5mm (¼in) apart. Brush the courgette with olive oil, ensuring it gets down into all the slits, and season with salt and pepper.

Place the courgette in the roasting tin with the tomato sauce and roast for 30–35 minutes until the courgette is starting to soften but is still firm.

SAUCE

Tip the tomato sauce into a large roasting tin and season with brown sugar and salt and pepper.

TOPPING

In a small pan, gently heat the cream with the rosemary for a few minutes (but don't allow to boil). Discard the rosemary.

ASSEMBLING

Serve the courgette and sauce on a plate, pour over the rosemary-infused cream, drizzle with a little extra virgin olive oil and scatter over the breadcrumbs.

ALTERNATIVE TIP
If you can't find gluten-free bread, you can swap the breadcrumbs for the buckwheat chunks on page 48.

ALTERNATIVE TIP
This recipe works very well
with other protein sources,
like pancakes, steamed
potatoes, beans and lentils.

COURGETTE (ZUCCHINI) WITH HUMMUS & RED (BELL) PEPPER SAUCE

INGREDIENTS

PROTEIN/CARB

200g (7oz) cannellini beans, drained
1 tablespoon olive oil
¼ teaspoon sea salt
1 teaspoon lemon juice

MAIN VEG

1 large courgette (zucchini)
extra virgin olive oil for brushing
sea salt and freshly ground
   black pepper, to taste

SAUCE

1 large red (bell) pepper, deseeded and
   chopped into large pieces
1 tablespoon olive oil
1 teaspoon cayenne pepper
2 garlic cloves, peeled
15g (½oz) almond flakes, soaked
¼ teaspoon salt
1 teaspoon apple cider vinegar

TOPPING

a sprinkle of fresh dill
a pinch of flaked almonds

METHOD

PROTEIN/CARB

Place all the ingredients in a blender and blend until smooth.

MAIN VEG

Preheat the oven to 200°C (400°F)/gas mark 6. Place the courgette in the roasting tin with the tomato sauce and roast for 30-35 minutes until the courgette starts to soften but remains firm. Remove from the oven and using a sharp knife, score the courgette widthways – each slice should cut about three-quarters of the way through and be spaced about 5mm (¼in) apart. Brush the courgette with olive oil, ensuring it gets down into all the slits, and season with salt and pepper.

SAUCE

Place the pepper in a roasting tin, drizzle with oil and roast in the oven for 30 minutes. Allow to cool, then place in a blender together with the remaining sauce ingredients, plus 2 tablespoons water, and blend until smooth.

ASSEMBLING

Spoon the sauce onto a plate with the hummus, then arrange the courgette on top and scatter over the toppings.

AUBERGINE (EGGPLANT) WITH SUN-DRIED TOMATOES & BUTTER BEAN HUMMUS

INGREDIENTS

PROTEIN/CARB

200g (7oz) butter beans, drained
2 tablespoons extra virgin olive oil
juice of ½ lemon
2 tablespoons sun-dried tomato pesto
½ garlic clove
sea salt, to taste

MAIN VEG

1 large aubergine (eggplant)
1 tablespoon extra virgin olive oil
sea salt and freshly ground
  black pepper, to taste

SAUCE

2 tablespoons sun-dried tomato pesto

TOPPING

a sprinkle of sesame seeds (better toasted)
a sprinkle of fresh flat-leaf parsley leaves

METHOD

PROTEIN/CARB

Place all the ingredients in a blender and blend until smooth.

MAIN VEG

Preheat the oven to 200°C (400°F)/gas mark 6. Place the aubergine directly on a baking tray (sheet) and bake for 45 minutes, until tender but not completely mushy. Transfer the aubergine to a chopping board or wire rack and let cool. Once cool enough to handle, remove the charred skin without damaging the flesh. Season the latter with 1 tablespoon extra virgin olive oil, and salt and pepper, to taste.

ASSEMBLING

Spoon the butter bean hummus onto a plate and lay the aubergine on top. Add dollops of sun-dried tomato pesto and finish with a sprinkle of sesame seeds and fresh parsley.

ALTERNATIVE TIP
Spice up the game by adding harissa paste or smoked sriracha to the pesto and hummus.

ALTERNATIVE TIP
To give the plate a Korean
twist, replace the tahini sauce
with the bulgogi sauce on
page 47.

FRIED AUBERGINE (EGGPLANT) WITH BLACK RICE & TAHINI SAUCE

INGREDIENTS

PROTEIN/CARB
120g (4¼oz) cooked black rice
1 tablespoon extra virgin olive oil
sea salt, to taste

MAIN VEG
1 large aubergine (eggplant)
3 tablespoons extra virgin olive oil
25g (1oz) chickpea (garbanzo bean) flour
1 tablespoon potato or corn starch
1 teaspoon sea salt
1 tablespoon extra virgin olive oil
sea salt and black pepper, to taste

SAUCE
1 tablespoon tahini
3½ tablespoons plant-based milk
  (rice or oat work best)
1 teaspoon smoked paprika
1 teaspoon maple syrup
sea salt, to taste

TOPPING
1 chilli pepper, deseeded and
  finely chopped
1 teaspoon sesame seeds
1 spring onion (scallion), finely chopped

METHOD

PROTEIN/CARB
In a bowl, mix the rice with the olive oil and salt, heat through and set aside but keep warm.

MAIN VEG
Preheat the oven to 200°C (400°F)/gas mark 6. Place the aubergine directly on a baking tray (sheet) and bake for 45 minutes–1 hour, until tender but not completely mushy. Transfer the aubergine to a chopping board or wire rack and let cool. Once cool enough to handle, remove the charred skin without damaging the flesh. Season the latter with 1 tablespoon extra virgin olive oil and salt and pepper, to taste.

Next, make the batter: place the flour and starch in a bowl and slowly pour in 1 tablespoon oil and 4 tablespoons water, beating with a whisk until you have a smooth, light batter (no lumps). Season with 1 teaspoon of salt. Dip the aubergine into the batter, to lightly coat, shaking off any excess.

Heat the remaining oil in a medium non-stick pan over a medium–high heat and, when hot, fry the aubergine for 1–2 minutes, then flip and cook for 1–2 minutes on the other side. Keep flipping until you reach your preferred crispiness (I prefer it a bit crispier).

SAUCE
Place all the ingredients in a blender and blend until smooth. Check the consistency – add a little more tahini until creamy enough for you.

ASSEMBLING
Spoon the rice onto a plate first and then add the aubergine. Drizzle with the sauce and scatter over the toppings.

AUBERGINE (EGGPLANT) WITH BASIL PESTO & BUCKWHEAT

INGREDIENTS

PROTEIN/CARB

60g (2½oz) cooked buckwheat
1 tablespoon olive oil
a pinch of sea salt

MAIN VEG

1 large aubergine (eggplant)
extra virgin olive oil for drizzling
sea salt and freshly ground black pepper
  to taste

SAUCE

a bunch of fresh basil
¾ tablespoon olive oil
1 tablespoon lemon juice
¼ teaspoon sea salt
1 teaspoon nutritional yeast
2 tablespoons broken pistachios

TOPPING

a sprinkle of broken pistachios
a sprinkle of fresh basil

METHOD

PROTEIN/CARB

Place the buckwheat in a deep pan, cover with 120ml (3¾fl oz) water and bring to the boil. Reduce to a simmer, cover and cook until the water has evaporated completely. Strain the buckwheat through a colander and rinse under hot water to remove the starchy and foxy bits. Set aside to drain, then when it's dry, transfer to a bowl and stir through the oil and season to taste.

MAIN VEG

Preheat the oven to 200°C (400°F)/gas mark 6. Slice the top off the aubergine and then slice lengthwise into thin 10mm (⅜in) layers. Discard the first and last layers (mostly the skin) and place the rest on a baking tray (sheet) lined with baking paper. Ensure they are not overlapping, then drizzle with oil, season with salt and pepper and bake for 20 minutes.

SAUCE

Place the basil, olive oil, lemon juice and salt with the nutritional yeast and half the pistachios in a blender and blend until smooth, then stir through the remaining nuts.

ASSEMBLING

Spoon the buckwheat onto a plate and top with a little sauce. Layer the aubergine on top and fill each layer with sauce. Finish with the remaining sauce and a sprinkle of broken pistachios and fresh basil.

 WATCH
THE ONLINE
RECIPE

ALTERNATIVE TIP
If you don't like buckwheat,
this recipe works well with
lentils and other small beans
or even breadcrumbs.

ALTERNATIVE TIP

If you don't want to use almonds, you can use cashews or shelled hemp seeds, or you can mix the nuts with sunflower seeds or oats, so it gets less expensive (but also less tasty).

AUBERGINE (EGGPLANT) 'PARMIGIANA' WITH TOMATO SAUCE & ALMOND 'RICOTTA'

INGREDIENTS

PROTEIN/CARB

100g (3½oz) blanched almonds
½ teaspoon sea salt
2 teaspoons lemon juice

MAIN VEG

1 large aubergine (eggplant)
1 tablespoon extra virgin olive oil
   for drizzling
sea salt and freshly ground
   black pepper to taste

SAUCE

2 tablespoons olive oil
½ shallot, finely chopped
200g (7fl oz) tomato sauce canned
   chopped tomatoes
½ teaspoon brown sugar
¼ teaspoon salt

TOPPING

a sprinkle of shelled hemp seeds
a sprinkle of fresh flat-leaf parsley

METHOD

PROTEIN/CARB

Place the almonds and salt with 150ml (5fl oz) water in a high-speed blender and blitz to combine. Transfer to a small saucepan and bring to the boil, then turn off the heat and add the lemon juice, stirring gently for a few minutes. Drain the liquid through a classic cheesecloth or just a colander or sieve into a bowl, then leave the almond 'ricotta' in the fridge overnight to release the rest of the water. Season further to taste.

MAIN VEG

Preheat the oven to 200°C (400°F)/gas mark 6. Slice the top off the aubergine and then slice lengthwise into thin 10mm (⅜in) layers. Discard the first and last layers (mostly the skin) and place the rest on a baking tray (sheet) lined with baking paper. Ensure they are not overlapping, then drizzle with oil (reserving half for later), season with salt and pepper and bake for 20 minutes.

SAUCE

Heat the olive oil in a pan over a medium heat and cook the shallot until transparent but not burned, then add the tomato, sugar and salt. Stir well and simmer for 20 minutes.

ASSEMBLING

Drizzle the remaining olive oil on the plate. Spoon a little sauce on top. Layer the aubergine on top and fill each layer with sauce. Finish with the remaining sauce, the almond 'ricotta' and the hemp seeds and parsley.

AUBERGINE (EGGPLANT) WITH BLACK BEANS & TRUFFLE SAUCE

INGREDIENTS

PROTEIN/CARB

1 tablespoon extra virgin olive oil

½ shallot, finely chopped

¼ courgette (zucchini), grated

120g (4¼oz) cooked black beans

¼ teaspoon sea salt

freshly ground black pepper, to taste

MAIN VEG

1 large aubergine (eggplant)

1 teaspoon extra virgin olive oil

sea salt and freshly ground black pepper,
  to taste

SAUCE

60ml (2fl oz) oat single (light) cream

1 teaspoon truffle oil

sea salt and freshly ground black pepper,
  to taste

TOPPING

a sprinkle of chilli flakes

a sprinkle of fresh flat-leaf parsley leaves

a sprinkle of hemp seeds

METHOD

PROTEIN/CARB

Heat the olive oil in a pan over a medium heat and cook the shallot until transparent but not burned, then add the courgette and cook until golden. Add the beans, stir well and heat through, then season with salt and pepper.

MAIN VEG

Preheat the oven to 200°C (400°F)/gas mark 6. Peel the aubergine and rub it with oil, salt and pepper. Place it on a baking tray (sheet) and bake for 30–35 minutes until tender, but still not completely mushy. Transfer to a chopping board or wire rack and let cool.

SAUCE

Place all the ingredients in a bowl and stir to combine.

ASSEMBLING

Spoon the sauce onto a plate, followed by the beans and lay the aubergine on top. Scatter over the chilli, parsley and hemp seeds and serve.

ALTERNATIVE TIP
This recipe works will many
different carbs and pulses, like
butter beans, rice, buckwheat,
quinoa, polenta (page 100) or
pancakes (page 79)

ALTERNATIVE TIP
This recipe works very well
with other protein sources,
like pancakes, steamed
potatoes, beans and lentils.

AUBERGINE (EGGPLANT) WITH YOGURT & CHICKPEAS (GARBANZO BEANS)

INGREDIENTS

PROTEIN/CARB

2.5cm (1 inch) piece cucumber
120g (4¼oz) cooked chickpeas
1 tablespoon extra virgin olive oil
sea salt and freshly ground black
   pepper, to taste

MAIN VEG

1 aubergine (eggplant)
1 tablespoon extra virgin olive oil
sea salt and freshly ground black
   pepper, to taste

SAUCE

2 tablespoons plant-based yogurt
   (unsweetened coconut is the best)
1 garlic clove, grated
¼ teaspoon sea salt

TOPPING

a sprinkle of chopped fresh dill
a pinch of sesame seeds

METHOD

PROTEIN/CARB

Slice the cucumber as thinly as you can (1mm-/ ¹⁄₁₆in thin), then add salt and press to release excess water. Set aside to drain and then place in a bowl with the chickpeas and oil, stir well and season to taste.

MAIN VEG

Preheat the oven to 200°C (400°F)/gas mark 6. Using a sharp knife, score the aubergine lengthways – each slice should cut about three-quarters of the way through and be spaced about 10mm (⅜in) apart. Brush the aubergine with olive oil, ensuring it gets down into all the slits, and season with salt and pepper. Transfer to a roasting tin and roast for 35–40 minutes until it starts to soften.

SAUCE

In a bowl, mix together the yogurt and garlic and season with salt.

ASSEMBLING

Spoon the sauce onto a plate, followed by the chickpeas (mix them together if you fancy), then add the aubergine and scatter over the toppings.

RADICCHIO WITH SUN-DRIED TOMATO PESTO & BLACK-EYED BEANS

INGREDIENTS

PROTEIN/CARB

120g (4¼oz) cooked black-eyed beans
1 tablespoon olive oil
1 tablespoon sun-dried tomato pesto
1 teaspoon lemon juice
sea salt, to taste

MAIN VEG

½ radicchio head, halved
1 teaspoon extra virgin olive oil
1 teaspoon brown sugar
sea salt and freshly ground black
  pepper, to taste

SAUCE

2 tablespoons sun-dried
  tomato pesto

TOPPING

a handful of pine nuts,
  toasted if liked
a handful of fresh flat-leaf
  parsley leaves

METHOD

PROTEIN/CARB

Place the beans in a bowl, add the rest of the ingredients and stir to combine.

MAIN VEG

Place a frying pan over a medium–high heat and, using tongs, lay the radicchio in the hot pan, cut-side down. Add the oil and sugar and sear on both sides for 10–15 minutes, flipping regularly with the tongs. Season to taste.

ASSEMBLING

Spoon the sun-dried tomato pesto onto a plate and add the beans. Place the radicchio on top and finish with a scatter of pine nuts and parsley.

ALTERNATIVE TIP
This recipe works well with all sorts of carbs, from lentils to quinoa, and roasted potatoes to polenta.

ALTERNATIVE TIP
If you don't have red lentils,
you can swap with other
types of lentils, beans or
green peas.

BAKED RADICCHIO WITH RED LENTILS & COCONUT

INGREDIENTS

PROTEIN/CARB

60g (2 ½ oz) red lentils
200ml (7fl oz) coconut milk
1 teaspoon ground turmeric
½ teaspoon minced ginger
1 garlic clove, minced
2 tablespoons coconut oil
½ teaspoon sea salt

MAIN VEG

1 radicchio head
1 teaspoon extra virgin olive oil
1 teaspoon brown sugar
sea salt and freshly ground black
  pepper, to taste

TOPPING

a sprinkle of toasted coconut
a sprinkle of finely chopped fresh
  tarragon or flat-leaf parsley leaves
sea salt and freshly ground
  black pepper, to taste

METHOD

PROTEIN/CARB

Rinse the lentils with fresh water before cooking to remove any dust or debris. Transfer to a pan together with the coconut milk, turmeric, ginger and garlic and simmer over a low heat for 15–20 minutes until tender. Keep the lentils nice and creamy as you have no sauce, so if they dry out too much, add a little extra coconut milk. Stir through the oil and salt after cooking.

MAIN VEG

Preheat the oven to 200°C (400°F)/gas mark 6. Slice off the bottom of the radicchio, then massage the oil, sugar, salt and pepper into its leaves. Transfer to a baking tray (sheet) lined with baking paper and bake for 25–30 minutes until tender.

ASSEMBLING

Spoon the lentils onto a plate and lay the radicchio on top, then scatter over the toasted coconut and tarragon or parsley and season to taste.

FRIED RADICCHIO WITH ALMOND 'RICOTTA' & BALSAMIC GLAZE

INGREDIENTS

PROTEIN/CARB

100g (3½oz) blanched almonds
½ teaspoon sea salt
2 teaspoons lemon juice

MAIN VEG

½ radicchio head, halved
1 teaspoon extra virgin olive oil
1 teaspoon balsamic vinegar
½ teaspoon brown sugar
sea salt and freshly ground black
  pepper, to taste

SAUCE

a drizzle of balsamic glaze

TOPPING

a handful of artichoke hearts, sliced
a handful of finely chopped fresh mint

METHOD

PROTEIN/CARB

Place the almonds and salt with 150ml (5fl oz) water in a high-speed blender and blitz to combine. Transfer to a small saucepan and bring to the boil, then turn off the heat and add the lemon juice, stirring gently for a few minutes. Drain the liquid through a classic cheesecloth or just a colander or sieve into a bowl, then leave the almond 'ricotta' in the fridge overnight to release the rest of the water. Taste and adjust the seasoning if necessary.

MAIN VEG

Place a frying pan over a medium–high heat and, using tongs, lay the radicchio in the hot pan, cut-side down. Add the oil, vinegar and sugar and sear on both sides for 10–15 minutes, flipping regularly with the tongs. Season to taste.

ASSEMBLING

Spoon the 'ricotta' onto a plate and lay the radicchio on top, together with the artichoke hearts. Drizzle with the balsamic glaze and scatter with fresh mint.

ALTERNATIVE TIP
If you don't have time to make the 'ricotta', this recipe works well with all sorts of creamy carbs, like hummus or a vegan spreadable cheeze.

ALTERNATIVE TIP

If you don't like the hot
sauce, this recipe works well
with almost any sauce, from
basil or sun-dried tomato
pestos to tahini sauce
and yogurt.

RADICCHIO WITH CHICKPEA (GARBANZO BEAN) PANCAKES & HOT SAUCE

INGREDIENTS

PROTEIN/CARB
70g (2¾oz) chickpea
  (garbanzo bean) flour
2 tablespoons potato or cornstarch
3 tablespoons extra virgin olive oil

MAIN VEG
½ radicchio head, halved
1 teaspoon extra virgin olive oil
1 teaspoon toasted sesame oil
½ teaspoon brown sugar
sea salt, to taste

SAUCE
2 tablespoons sriracha sauce or
  another hot sauce of your choice

TOPPING
a sprinkle of toasted sesame seeds
1 spring onion (scallion),
  finely chopped

METHOD

PROTEIN/CARB
Tip the flour and starch into a bowl or blender. Slowly pour in 2 tablespoons oil and 210ml (7½fl oz) water, beating with a whisk until you have a smooth, light batter (no lumps).

Heat 1 tablespoon oil in a non-stick frying pan over a medium–high heat. Pour in the batter, tilting the pan a little to ensure a thin and even layer. When the sides are crispy enough and the top is bubbly, use a spatula to gently flip the pancake and cook the other side. Keep flipping until you reach your preferred crispiness – I like it pretty crispy, so I cook it for a bit longer. You can also make smaller pancakes (like the ones in the picture) by pouring only a third of the mixture into the pan at a time.

MAIN VEG
Place a frying pan over a medium–high heat and, using tongs, lay the radicchio in the hot pan, cut-side down. Add the oils and sugar and sear on both sides for 10–15 minutes, flipping regularly with the tongs. Season to taste.

ASSEMBLING
Spoon the sauce onto a plate, lay the pancakes on top and then add the radicchio. Drizzle with hot sauce and finish with a sprinkle of sesame seeds and spring onion.

WATCH
THE ONLINE
RECIPE

ROASTED FENNEL WITH BLACK RICE & MUSTARD SAUCE

INGREDIENTS

PROTEIN/CARB
120g (4¼oz) cooked black rice
1 tablespoon extra virgin olive oil
a sprinkle of fresh thyme
sea salt and freshly ground black pepper,
  to taste

MAIN VEG
1 tablespoon extra virgin olive oil plus
  extra for drizzling
juice of ½ lemon
1 teaspoon English mustard
a pinch of brown sugar
1 large fennel, topped, tailed and sliced
  in half lengthwise
sea salt and freshly ground black pepper,
  to taste

SAUCE
3–4 tablespoons vegan milk (rice, soya
  or oat)
1 tablespoon tahini
¼ teaspoon sea salt
1 teaspoon English mustard
juice of ½ lemon

TOPPING
a sprinkle of almond flakes
a sprinkle of fresh thyme
a handful of pomegranate seeds

METHOD

PROTEIN/CARB
Place the rice in a bowl, stir through the oil and thyme and season
to taste.

MAIN VEG
Preheat the oven to 200°C (400°F)/gas mark 6. Place the oil,
lemon juice, mustard and sugar in a bowl, season with salt and
pepper and mix well. Place the fennel on a sheet of baking paper,
cover with the marinade and wrap up tightly.

Place the parcel on a baking tray (sheet) lined with baking paper
and allow to bake for 15 minutes. Then, open the parcel, drizzle
with extra olive oil, sprinkle with salt and bake for a further 30
minutes, until tender.

SAUCE
Place all the ingredients in a blender and blend until smooth.
Check the consistency; add more tahini for a smoother sauce or
milk for a runnier one.

ASSEMBLING
Spoon the sauce onto a plate and add the rice. Arrange the
fennel on top and scatter over the almond flakes, thyme and
pomegranate seeds.

ALTERNATIVE TIP
As well as with rice, this
recipe works with other carbs,
like chickpeas or beans or
buckwheat pancakes
(page 167).

ALTERNATIVE TIP
As well as the pancake, this recipe can work with other carbs, like chickpeas or beans or buckwheat.

ROASTED FENNEL WITH CHICKPEA (GARBANZO BEAN) PANCAKE & TOMATO

INGREDIENTS

MAIN VEG

1 tablespoon olive oil

1 teaspoon cider vinegar

a pinch of brown sugar

1 large fennel, topped, tailed and sliced in half lengthwise

sea salt and freshly ground black pepper, to taste

PROTEIN/CARB

50g (2oz) chickpea (garbanzo bean) flour

2 tablespoons potato or corn starch

2 tablespoons extra virgin olive oil

2 teaspoons sea salt

a handful of fresh oregano

SAUCE

1 tablespoon olive oil

½ shallot, finely chopped

200g (7fl oz) canned chopped tomatoes

1 teaspoon brown sugar

¼ teaspoon sea salt

TOPPING

a handful of fresh basil

a sprinkle of pine nuts

a handful of pitted black olives

METHOD

MAIN VEG

Preheat the oven to 200°C (400°F)/gas mark 6. Place the oil, cider vinegar and sugar in a bowl, season with salt and pepper and mix well. Place the fennel on a sheet of baking paper, cover with the marinade and wrap it tightly with the paper.

Place the parcel on a baking tray (sheet) lined with baking paper and bake for 15 minutes, then open the open the parcel, drizzle with extra olive oil, sprinkle with salt and bake for a further 30 minutes, until tender.

PROTEIN/CARB

Tip the flour and starch into a bowl. Slowly pour in 2 tablespoons oil and 120ml (3¾fl oz) water, beating with a whisk until you have a smooth, light batter (no lumps). Sprinkle over the salt and oregano and mix well.

Heat 1 tablespoon oil in a non-stick frying pan over a medium–high heat. Pour in the batter, tilting the pan a little to ensure a thin and even layer. When the sides are crispy enough and the top is bubbly, use a spatula to gently flip the pancake and cook the other side. Keep flipping until you reach your preferred crispiness – I like it pretty crispy, so I cook it for a bit longer. You can also make smaller pancakes (like the one in the picture) by pouring only a third of the mixture into the pan at a time.

SAUCE

Heat the olive oil in a pan over a medium heat and cook the shallot until transparent but not burned, then add the tomato, sugar and salt. Stir well and simmer for 20 minutes.

ASSEMBLING

Spoon the sauce onto a plate and lay the pancake on top, followed by the fennel and toppings.

ROASTED FENNEL WITH BUTTER BEAN HUMMUS & BASIL PESTO

INGREDIENTS

PROTEIN/CARB
120g (4¼oz) cooked butter beans
2 tablespoons olive oil
¼ teaspoon sea salt
1 teaspoon lemon juice

MAIN VEG
1 tablespoon extra virgin olive oil plus
  extra; for drizzling
juice of ½ lemon
a pinch of vegetable bouillon powder
a pinch of brown sugar
1 large fennel, topped, tailed
  and sliced in half lengthwise
sea salt and freshly ground black pepper,
  to taste

SAUCE
a bunch of fresh basil
3–4 tablespoons olive oil
1 teaspoon lemon juice
¼ teaspoon sea salt
1 teaspoon nutritional yeast
2 tablespoons almond flakes

TOPPING
a sprinkle of almond flakes
a sprinkle of fresh basil leaves

METHOD

PROTEIN/CARB
Place all the ingredients with 1 tablespoon water in a blender and blend until smooth.

MAIN VEG
Preheat the oven to 200°C (400°F)/gas mark 6. Place the oil, lemon juice, bouillon powder and sugar in a bowl, season with salt and pepper and mix well. Place the fennel on a sheet of baking paper, cover with the marinade and fold the paper over to wrap it up tightly.

Place the parcel on a baking tray (sheet) lined with baking paper and bake for 15 minutes, then open up the parcel, drizzle with extra olive oil, sprinkle with salt and bake for a further 30 minutes, until tender.

SAUCE
Place the basil, olive oil, lemon juice and salt with the nutritional yeast and half the almond flakes in a blender and blend until smooth, then stir through the remaining nuts.

ASSEMBLING
Spoon the sauce and hummus onto a plate, top with the fennel and scatter over the almond flakes and fresh basil.

ALTERNATIVE TIP
If you don't have the time to
make the hummus or pesto,
you can buy them.

ALTERNATIVE TIP
If you don't have rice, you can replace it with quinoa, oats or buckwheat, though cooking times will vary.

SMOKED FENNEL WITH RADICCHIO RISOTTO & SOURED CREAM

INGREDIENTS

MAIN VEG
1 tablespoon extra virgin olive oil plus
   extra for drizzling
½ teaspoon brown sugar
1 tablespoon ketchup
1 tablespoon smoked paprika
1 teaspoon sea salt
1 fennel, topped, tailed and sliced in
   half lengthwise

PROTEIN/CARB
2 tablespoons extra virgin olive oil
½ shallot, finely chopped
1 garlic clove, finely chopped
½ radicchio head, finely chopped
1 teaspoon vegetable bouillon powder
60g (2 ½ oz) risotto rice
120ml (3¾fl oz) hot water
1 teaspoon sea salt
sea salt and freshly ground black pepper,
   to taste

SAUCE
2 tablespoons vegan single
   (light) cream (oat)
1 teaspoon lemon juice

TOPPING
a sprinkle of finely chopped
   radicchio head
a sprinkle of fresh flat-leaf parsley

METHOD

MAIN VEG
Preheat the oven to 200°C (400°F)/gas mark 6. Place the oil, sugar, ketchup, smoked paprika and salt in a bowl and mix well. Place the fennel on a sheet of baking paper, cover with the marinade and fold the paper over to wrap it up tightly.

Place the parcel on a baking tray (sheet) lined with baking paper and bake for 15 minutes, then open up the parcel, drizzle with extra olive oil, sprinkle with salt and bake for a further 30 minutes, until tender.

PROTEIN/CARB
Heat the oil in a pan over a medium heat and fry the shallot and garlic for 10–15 minutes until softened, then add the radicchio and fry for a further 10 minutes.

Place the vegetable bouillon powder in a jug, pour over 120ml (3¾fl oz) boiling water and stir to dissolve. Add the rice to the pan and turn up the heat – the rice will now begin to lightly fry, so keep stirring (after a minute it will look slightly translucent). Add the bouillon a ladle at a time and keep stirring. Turn the heat down to a simmer, add the salt and keep adding the stock (broth), slowly slowly, stirring often, for around 15 minutes until the rice is tender and creamy. Season to taste with salt and pepper.

SAUCE
In a bowl, mix together the vegan cream with the lemon juice.

ASSEMBLING
Spoon the risotto onto a plate and lay the fennel on top. Drizzle over the sauce and finish with the toppings.

YOGURT-COATED BAKED BROCCOLI WITH CURRIED RED LENTILS

INGREDIENTS

PROTEIN/CARB
60g (2½oz) red lentils
200ml (7fl oz) coconut milk
1 teaspoon curry powder
1 teaspoon smoked paprika
1 garlic clove, finely chopped
¼ red (bell) pepper,
  deseeded and finely chopped
2 tablespoons coconut oil
½ teaspoon sea salt

MAIN VEG
3 tablespoons vegan yogurt (soya
  works best)
1 teaspoon sugar
1 tablespoon garlic powder
1 teaspoon sea salt
1 small head of broccoli (remove most
  of the stalk)
1 tablespoon extra virgin olive oil

TOPPING
a sprinkle of toasted coconut
a sprinkle of fresh coriander (cilantro)
a sprinkle of chilli flakes
sea salt and freshly ground black pepper,
  to taste

METHOD

PROTEIN/CARB
Rinse the lentils with fresh water before cooking to remove any dust or debris. Transfer to a pan together with the coconut milk, curry powder, smoked paprika, garlic and pepper and simmer over a low heat for 15–20 minutes until tender. Keep the lentils nice and creamy as you have no sauce, so if they dry out too much, add a little extra coconut milk. Stir through the oil and salt after cooking.

MAIN VEG
Preheat the oven to 200°C (400°F)/gas mark 6. Place the yogurt, sugar, garlic powder and salt in a bowl and mix well. Place the broccoli on a sheet of baking paper, cover with the marinade and fold the paper over to wrap it up tightly. Allow to marinate for 20 minutes (or ideally leave in the fridge overnight to marinate).

Place the parcel on a baking tray (sheet) lined with baking paper and bake for 20 minutes, then open up the parcel, drizzle with extra virgin olive oil, sprinkle with salt and bake for a further 20 minutes, until tender.

ASSEMBLING
Spoon the lentils onto a plate and arrange the broccoli on top. Scatter with coconut, coriander (cilantro) and chilli flakes and season to taste.

ALTERNATIVE TIP

If you don't have red lentils, replace them with green peas, buckwheat, quinoa or even rice.

ALTERNATIVE TIP
If you don't have black
rice, you can use a more
classic Japanese white rice or
basmati, or even buckwheat
or quinoa.

BROCCOLI WITH A MISO GLAZE & BLACK RICE

INGREDIENTS

PROTEIN/CARB
60g (2½oz) black rice
1 teaspoon lemon juice
½ teaspoon ground ginger
1 garlic clove, finely chopped

MAIN VEG
½ large head of broccoli, sliced in
    half lengthwise

SAUCE
4 tablespoons miso
4 tablespoons soy sauce
2 tablespoons rice vinegar
2 tablespoons maple syrup or rice syrup
2 teaspoons toasted sesame oil

TOPPING
a sprinkle of toasted sesame seeds
1 spring onion (scallion), finely chopped
a sprinkle of nori flakes
sea salt and freshly ground black pepper,
    to taste

METHOD

PROTEIN/CARB
Place the rice in a pan with the lemon juice, ginger and garlic and cover with 200ml (7fl oz) water. Bring to the boil over a medium heat, then reduce to a simmer, cover and cook for around 45 minutes or until you have your preferred texture (black rice will always be pretty chewy). Top up with more water if needed.

MAIN VEG
Preheat the oven to 200°C (400°F)/gas mark 6. First make the sauce (see below). Place the broccoli in the bag with the sauce (ensuring it is evenly coated). Leave to marinate for 20 minutes (or ideally leave in the fridge overnight).

Place the broccoli on a baking tray (sheet) lined with baking paper and coat again. Bake for 35–40 minutes until tender.

SAUCE
Place all the ingredients in a bowl and mix together, then transfer to a resealable bag.

ASSEMBLING
Spoon the rice onto a plate, lay the broccoli on top, scatter over the toppings and season to taste.

FRIED BROCCOLI WITH PEA CREAM & CRISPY, SMOKY POTATOES

INGREDIENTS

PROTEIN/CARB

1 large potato, peeled
1 tablespoon olive oil
1 teaspoon smoked paprika
1 teaspoon maple syrup
sea salt and freshly ground black pepper,
  to taste

MAIN VEG

½ large broccoli, sliced in half
  lengthwise
60g (2 ½ oz) chickpea
  (garbanzo bean) flour
2 tablespoons potato or corn starch
2 tablespoons olive oil
3 tablespoons vegetable oil

SAUCE

60g (2½oz) frozen green peas
50ml (2fl oz) single (light) vegan cream
1 tablespoon olive oil
sea salt and freshly ground black pepper,
  to taste

TOPPING

a sprinkle of fresh lemon thyme
sea salt and freshly ground black pepper,
  to taste

METHOD

PROTEIN/CARB

Preheat the oven to 200°C (400°F)/gas mark 6. Using a vegetable peeler, peel the potato into long, thin strips, then place on a baking tray (sheet) lined with baking paper and drizzle with olive oil, smoked paprika and maple syrup. Season with salt and pepper and bake for 20 minutes.

MAIN VEG

Place the broccoli on a baking tray (sheet) lined with baking paper, drizzle with olive oil (reserving half for later) and fold the paper over to wrap it up tightly. Bake for 15 minutes until softer, then open the parcel and bake for a further 15 minutes.

Tip the flour and starch into a bowl or blender. Slowly pour in the remaining olive oil and 120ml (3¾fl oz) water, beating with a whisk until you have a smooth, light batter (no lumps). Heat the vegetable oil in a medium non-stick pan. Remove the broccoli from the oven and, using tongs, dip the cut side in the batter, ensuring it's evenly coated. Transfer the broccoli to the hot pan and fry, cut-side down, for a few minutes until crispy.

SAUCE

Defrost the peas by steaming them for a few minutes, then place with all the other ingredients in a blender and blend until smooth.

ASSEMBLING

Spoon the sauce onto a plate, followed by the crispy potatoes. Place the broccoli on top, scatter with lemon thyme and season to taste.

ALTERNATIVE TIP
If you want to make this
recipe very naughty, replace
the pea cream with mayo or
ketchup, or both.

ALTERNATIVE TIP

If you don't have chickpeas (garbanzo beans), you can use butter beans, black beans, black-eyed beans or even kidney beans.

ROASTED BROCCOLI WITH CHICKPEA (GARBANZO BEAN) HUMMUS & HARISSA TOMATO SAUCE

INGREDIENTS

PROTEIN/CARB

120g (4¼oz) cooked chickpeas
 (garbanzo beans)
1–2 tablespoons lemon juice
2 tablespoons olive oil
1 tablespoon finely chopped fresh mint
1 tablespoon tahini
peppercorns
sea salt and freshly ground black pepper

MAIN VEG

½ large head of broccoli, sliced in
 half lengthwise
1 tablespoon olive oil
sea salt, to taste

SAUCE

1 tablespoon olive oil
½ shallot, finely chopped
200g (7fl oz) passata
1 tablespoon harissa paste
1 teaspoon brown sugar
¼ teaspoon salt

TOPPING

a drizzle of extra virgin olive oil
a sprinkle of fresh mint
a sprinkle of smoked paprika
1 teaspoon hulled hemp seeds

METHOD

PROTEIN/CARB

Place the chickpeas in a blender with the lemon juice, olive oil, tahini, fresh mint and peppercorns and blend until smooth (add a teaspoon of water if necessary). Season to taste.

MAIN VEG

Preheat the oven to 200°C (400°F)/gas mark 6. Place the broccoli on a baking tray (sheet) lined with baking paper, cut-side up. Drizzle with olive oil, sprinkle with salt and bake for 45 minutes until tender.

SAUCE

Heat the olive oil in a pan over a medium heat and sauté the shallot until transparent but not burned, then add the tomato, harissa paste, sugar and salt. Stir well and simmer for 20 minutes.

ASSEMBLING

Spoon the sauce onto a plate with the hummus. Lay the broccoli on top, drizzle with olive oil and scatter over the toppings.

ALTERNATIVE TIP
If you don't have the time to
make the yellow peas, you can use
cooked butter beans, cannellini
beans, lentils or chickpeas.

BAKED CAULIFLOWER WITH YELLOW PEAS & TAHINI SAUCE

INGREDIENTS

MAIN VEG

1 small cauliflower, de-stalked

1 tablespoon olive oil

1 teaspoon salt

30g (1oz) buckwheat flour

125ml (4fl oz) rice milk (or other plant-based milk)

1 teaspoon garlic powder

1 teaspoon ground turmeric

sea salt and freshly ground black pepper

PROTEIN/CARB

225g (8oz) yellow split peas

1 teaspoon vegetable bouillon powder

1 teaspoon ground cumin

1 teaspoon ground turmeric

1 tablespoon olive oil

sea salt and freshly ground black pepper, to taste

SAUCE

4 tablespoons rice milk (or other plant-based milk)

2 tablespoons tahini

a pinch of salt

1 tablespoon nutritional yeast (optional)

TOPPING

a drizzle of extra virgin olive oil

a sprinkle of finely chopped fresh dill

1 teaspoon sesame seeds

METHOD

MAIN VEG

Preheat the oven to 200°C (400°F)/gas mark 6. Place the cauliflower on a baking tray (sheet) lined with baking paper. Drizzle with oil, sprinkle with salt and bake for 25 minutes.

Meanwhile, prepare the coating: in a bowl, mix the flour, milk, garlic powder and turmeric. After 25 minutes, remove the cauliflower from the oven and pour the mix on top, ensuring it is thoroughly and evenly coated, then return to the oven for a further 25 minutes, until golden and crispy. Before plating, remove any excess baked buckwheat from the bottom of the cauliflower (some of it may have burned) and season to taste. Before serving, drain the excess water, add the olive oil and season to taste.

PROTEIN/CARB

Place the peas in a pan, cover with 750ml (1¾pints) water and bring to a simmer over a medium heat. Stir in the bouillon powder and spices, then reduce the heat slightly and cook for approximately 1 hour. Check the peas while they are cooking and add more water if necessary. Keep the water level just above the peas.

SAUCE

Place all the ingredients in a blender and blend until smooth. Check the consistency – add extra milk if the sauce is too thick or tahini if it is too runny.

ASSEMBLING

Spoon the sauce onto a plate with the peas. Arrange the cauliflower on top, drizzle with extra virgin olive oil and scatter over the toppings.

CAULIFLOWER, POLENTA & BBQ SAUCE

INGREDIENTS

SAUCE/MARINADE
½ small onion
1 garlic clove
1 tablespoon olive oil
1 teaspoon sea salt
3 tablespoons ketchup
1 teaspoon English mustard
1 teaspoon Worcestershire sauce
1 tablespoon molasses or brown sugar
1 tablespoon maple syrup
1 tablespoon cider vinegar or lemon
 juice
OR
5 tablespoons of BBQ sauce
1 tablespoon vegetable oil
1 tablespoon maple syrup

MAIN VEG
1 small cauliflower, de-stalked
1 tablespoon vegetable oil

PROTEIN/CARB
400ml (14fl oz) vegetable milk
 (rice or oat)
100g (3½oz) quick polenta
1 tablespoon vegan butter or margarine
sea salt and freshly ground black pepper

TOPPING
a drizzle of extra virgin olive oil
1 teaspoon hulled hemp seeds
sea salt and freshly ground black pepper

METHOD

SAUCE
Place the onion and garlic in a blender and purée. Heat the olive oil in a pan over a medium heat and sauté the purée for about 5 minutes, being careful not to burn it. Take the pan off the heat and stir through all the remaining ingredients. If using BBQ sauce, vegetable oil and maple syrup instead, mix together in a bowl and stir through. Set aside to cool.

MAIN VEG
Preheat the oven to 200°C (400°F)/gas mark 6. Place the cauliflower on a baking tray (sheet) lined with baking paper and cover in half the sauce (reserving the rest), ensuring it's evenly coated. Wrap it up tightly into a paper parcel (you can marinate it overnight but it's not essential), and bake for 30 minutes, then open up the parcel and bake for a further 15 minutes until crispy on the outside.

PROTEIN/CARB
Place the milk in a pan and bring to the boil over a medium heat. Slowly pour in the polenta and stir for about 3 minutes, until the mixture thickens. Take off the heat, stir through the vegan butter and season to taste.

ASSEMBLING
Spoon the polenta onto a plate and pour over the reserved sauce. Arrange the cauliflower on top, drizzle with extra virgin olive oil, scatter with hemp seeds and season to taste.

ALTERNATIVE TIP
This recipe works with almost
any carb. If you don't have
polenta around, you can
use hummus, buckwheat,
roasted potatoes, quinoa,
rice or beans.

ALTERNATIVE TIP
This recipe works very well
with many different sauces,
like hot sauce, ketchup or the
sriracha sauce on page 104.

FRIED CAULIFLOWER WITH PEAS & CABBAGE SLAW

INGREDIENTS

PROTEIN/CARB

100g (3½oz) frozen green peas

50g (2oz) red cabbage, finely chopped

½ a small pepper, finely chopped

1 tablespoon olive oil

a pinch of sea salt

MAIN VEG

½ cauliflower head

1 tablespoon olive oil

½ teaspoon salt

½ cup chickpea (garbanzo bean) flour

½ cup corn starch

3 tablespoons rolled oats

250ml (9fl oz) sparkling water

500ml (18fl oz) vegetable oil

SAUCE

4 tablespoons vegan mayo

4 tablespoons vegan single
  (light) cream

1 teaspoon English mustard

½ teaspoon salt

TOPPING

1 tablespoon broken cashew nuts

a handful of fresh coriander (cilantro)

METHOD

PROTEIN/CARB

Defrost the peas by steaming them for 4–5 minutes, then mix in a bowl with the cabbage, pepper, olive oil and salt.

MAIN VEG

Preheat the oven to 200°C (400°F)/gas mark 6. Slice the cauliflower to make a 5cm- (2in-) thick 'steak'. Reserve the remaining trimmed florets for another day – you can use them to make cauliflower rice. Place the cauliflower on a baking tray (sheet) lined with baking paper. Drizzle with olive oil and salt and bake for 25 minutes, then set aside to cool.

Meanwhile, prepare the batter: place the flour and starch in a bowl with the sea salt and whisk in the sparkling water when you are ready to use. Place the rolled oats on a shallow plate next to the batter. Place the vegetable oil in a saucepan or deep frying pan (skillet) over a medium–high heat and, when hot, dip the cauliflower into the batter to lightly coat (shaking off any excess batter) and then into the oats.

Fry the cauliflower for 2–3 minutes, then flip over and cook for 1–2 minutes on the other side. When evenly cooked, transfer to a plate lined with kitchen paper to soak up any excess oil.

SAUCE

Combine all the ingredients in a bowl. Add half the sauce to the bowl of peas and cabbage and stir through. Reserve the rest.

ASSEMBLING

Spoon the slaw onto a plate and place the cauliflower on top. Drizzle with the remaining sauce and scatter over the toppings.

ROASTED CAULIFLOWER WITH CORN & CINNAMON TOMATO SAUCE

INGREDIENTS

PROTEIN/CARB
100g (3½oz) fresh sweetcorn

MAIN VEG
½ cauliflower, halved
1 tablespoon olive oil
1 teaspoon lemon juice
¼ teaspoon salt

SAUCE
1 tablespoon olive oil
½ shallot, finely chopped
1 garlic clove, finely chopped
200g (7oz) canned chopped tomatoes
1 teaspoon brown sugar
¼ teaspoon salt
1 teaspoon ground cinnamon

TOPPING
a sprinkle of fresh flat-leaf parsley

METHOD

MAIN VEG
Preheat the oven to 200°C (400°F)/gas mark 6. Place the cauliflower on a baking tray (sheet) lined with baking paper, drizzle with oil and lemon juice and sprinkle with salt and bake in the oven for 30 minutes. Meanwhile, make the sauce (see below).

Using tongs, transfer the cauliflower to a frying pan (skillet), cut-side down. Add the corn, pour over the sauce and cook, covered, for a further 15 minutes.

SAUCE
Heat the olive oil in a pan over a medium heat and sauté the shallot and garlic until transparent but not burned. Add 100ml (3½fl oz) water, along with the tomato sauce, sugar, salt and ground cinnamon, then stir well, cover with a lid and let simmer for 30 minutes.

ASSEMBLING
Spoon the sauce onto a plate and lay the cauliflower on top. Scatter over the fresh parsley and serve.

WATCH
THE ONLINE
RECIPE

ALTERNATIVE TIP
This recipe works very well
with many different carbs.
You can replace the corn
with lentils, beans, peas,
steamed potatoes or even
chunky breadcrumbs.

ALTERNATIVE TIP
The recipe also works
beautifully with quinoa
instead of rice.

ROASTED CAULIFLOWER WITH LEMON & SEAWEED BLACK RICE

INGREDIENTS

PROTEIN/CARB
50g (2oz) black rice

juice of ½ lemon

10g (¼oz) dulse seaweed or nori
 (the sushi ones)

MAIN VEG
juice of ½ lemon

1 tablespoon olive oil plus extra
 for drizzling (optional)

2 garlic cloves, finely chopped

1 teaspoon sea salt

½ purple cauliflower, halved

SAUCE
50g (2oz) cashews nuts, soaked

1 teaspoon tamari soy sauce

TOPPING
a sprinkle of sesame seeds

a handful of radish sprouts (optional)
 or fresh flat-leaf parsley

1 spring onion (scallion), finely chopped

METHOD

PROTEIN/CARB
Place the rice in a pan with the lemon juice and seaweed and cover with 200ml (7fl oz) water. Bring to the boil over a medium heat, then reduce to a simmer, cover and cook for around 45 minutes or until you have your preferred texture (one thing to keep in mind is that black rice will always be pretty chewy) so top up with more water if needed.

MAIN VEG
Place the lemon juice, olive oil, garlic and salt in a resealable bag and add the cauliflower steaks, ensuring they are thoroughly coated. Set aside to marinate for at least 15–20 minutes.

Preheat the oven to 200°C (400°F)/gas mark 6. Place the cauliflower on a baking tray (sheet) lined with baking paper and cover in the marinade. Wrap the paper up tightly into a parcel and cook in the oven for 15 minutes, then uncover and baste again with the marinade to keep it moist (drizzle with more olive oil if needed). Bake for another 20–30 minutes until tender but not burned.

SAUCE
Place the cashew nuts with the tamari sauce and 100ml (3½fl oz) water in a blender and blend until smooth.

TOPPING
Spoon the rice onto a plate and arrange the roasted cauliflower on top. Drizzle over the sauce and scatter over the toppings.

BAKED CAULIFLOWER WITH QUINOA & SAFFRON BÉCHAMEL

INGREDIENTS

PROTEIN/CARB
120g (4¼oz) cooked quinoa

MAIN VEG
1 tablespoon olive oil plus extra,
  for drizzling (optional)
1 tablespoon oat cream
2 garlic cloves, finely chopped
1 teaspoon brown sugar
2 bay leaves
¼ teaspoon salt
½ cauliflower, halved

SAUCE
1 tablespoon olive oil
½ shallot, finely chopped
1 garlic clove, finely chopped
2 bay leaves
100ml (3½fl oz) oat cream
¼ teaspoon salt
a pinch of saffron
1 tablespoon gluten-free flour of your
  choice (oat, buckwheat or rice)

TOPPING
a sprinkle of fresh flat-leaf parsley
a sprinkle of saffron
sea salt and freshly ground pink pepper,
  to taste

METHOD

MAIN VEG
Place the olive oil, oat cream, garlic, sugar, bay leaves and salt in a resealable bag and add the cauliflower steaks, ensuring they are coated. Set aside to marinate for at least 15–20 minutes.

Preheat the oven to 200°C (400°F)/gas mark 6. Place the cauliflower on a baking tray (sheet) lined with baking paper and cover in the marinade. Wrap the paper up tightly into a parcel and cook in the oven for 30 minutes, then uncover and baste again with the marinade to keep it moist (drizzle with more olive oil if needed). Bake for a further 15 minutes until tender but not burned.

SAUCE
Heat the olive oil in a pan over a medium heat and sauté the shallot and garlic until transparent but not burned. Add the bay leaves and oat cream, reduce the heat, cover and simmer for 5 minutes. Sift in the flour and mix well until slightly thickened and completely smooth. Add the salt and a pinch of saffron.

ASSEMBLING
Mix the quinoa with 2 tablespoons of the sauce and then spoon onto a plate. Place the cauliflower on top and drizzle over the remaining sauce. Finish with a sprinkle of parsley and saffron and season to taste.

ALTERNATIVE TIP
This recipe works very well with many different carbs. You can replace the quinoa with lentils, beans, hummus, steamed potatoes or even couscous.

ALTERNATIVE TIP
This recipe works very well with many different sauces, not just tomato, but also the mushroom gravy on page 196, the béchamel on page 139 and even the red wine sauce on page 199.

ROASTED RED CABBAGE WITH POTATOES & TOMATO SAUCE

INGREDIENTS

PROTEIN/CARB

1 large potato, peeled and
 chopped into 2.5cm (1in) cubes
2 teaspoons olive oil
1/2 teaspoon sea salt
sea salt and freshly ground
 black pepper, to taste

MAIN VEG

2 tablespoons extra virgin
 olive oil plus extra, for drizzling
1 teaspoon lemon juice
a handful of fresh rosemary
1 garlic clove, finely chopped
1 teaspoon brown sugar
1 teaspoon sea salt
1/2 small red cabbage, outer
 leaves removed and halved

SAUCE

1 tablespoon olive oil
1/2 shallot, finely chopped
200g (7oz) canned chopped
 tomatoes
1 teaspoon brown sugar
1/4 teaspoon salt

TOPPING

a drizzle of extra virgin olive oil
a sprinkle of chilli flakes

METHOD

PROTEIN/CARB

Preheat the oven to 200°C (400°F)/gas mark 6. Spread the potato cubes out over a baking tray (sheet) lined with baking paper, drizzle with olive oil and sprinkle with salt. Bake for 30 minutes until crispy, then season to taste.

MAIN VEG

Place the olive oil, lemon juice, rosemary, garlic, sugar and salt in a resealable bag and add the cabbage halves, ensuring they are thoroughly coated. Set aside to marinate for at least 15–20 minutes (ideally overnight).

Preheat the oven to 200°C (400°F)/gas mark 6. Place the cabbage on a baking tray (sheet) lined with baking paper and cover in the marinade. Wrap up tightly in the baking paper and cook in the oven for 30 minutes, then uncover and baste again with the marinade to keep it moist (drizzle with more oil if needed). Bake for a further 15 minutes until tender.

SAUCE

Heat the olive oil in a pan over a medium heat and sauté the shallot until transparent but not burned. Add the tomatoes, along with the sugar and salt and stir well, then cover with a lid and let simmer for 20 minutes.

ASSEMBLING

Spoon half the tomato sauce onto a plate and top with the potatoes. Lay the cabbage on top and pour over the remaining sauce. Finish with a drizzle of extra virgin olive oil and a sprinkle of chilli flakes.

SMOKED ROASTED CABBAGE WITH GREEN PEAS & OAT CREAM

INGREDIENTS

MAIN VEG

2 tablespoons extra virgin olive oil
  plus extra, for drizzling (optional)
1 tablespoon cider vinegar
1 tablespoon maple syrup
1 tablespoon smoked paprika
1 garlic clove, finely chopped
1 teaspoon sea salt
½ small red cabbage, outer leaves
  removed and halved

PROTEIN/CARB

60g (2½oz) frozen green peas
1 tablespoon olive oil
sea salt and freshly ground black pepper,
  to taste

SAUCE

50ml vegan single (light) cream (oat) or
  sour cream (even better)

TOPPING

a sprinkle of sesame seeds
a sprinkle of fresh coriander (cilantro)
sea salt and freshly ground black pepper,
  to taste

METHOD

MAIN VEG

Preheat the oven to 200°C (400°F)/gas mark 6. Place the olive oil, cider vinegar, maple syrup, paprika, garlic, and salt in a resealable bag and add the cabbage halves, ensuring they are thoroughly coated. Set aside to marinate for at least 15–20 minutes (ideally overnight).

Place the cabbage on a baking tray (sheet) lined with baking paper and cover in the marinade. Wrap the paper up tightly into a parcel and cook in the oven for 30 minutes, then uncover and baste again with the marinade to keep it moist (drizzle with more olive oil if needed). Bake for a further 15 minutes until tender.

PROTEIN/CARB

Defrost the peas by steaming them for 4–5 minutes, then transfer to a bowl, drizzle with olive oil and season with salt and pepper.

ASSEMBLING

Pour the single (light) or sour cream into a wide shallow bowl and spoon over the peas. Place the cabbage on top and finish with a final drizzle of cream and a scatter of sesame seeds and fresh coriander (cilantro) leaves. Season to taste.

ALTERNATIVE TIP
This recipe works very well with many different pulses, not just peas, so try with chickpeas (garbanzo bean), black beans or even lentils.

ALTERNATIVE TIP
This recipe is very unique, but, if you don't like the hot sauce, you can use ketchup, or replace the mayo with a healthier version, like the avocado & miso sauce on page 175.

FRIED POINTED CABBAGE WITH CHICKPEA (GARBANZO BEAN) PANCAKE & HOT SAUCE

INGREDIENTS

PROTEIN/CARB
50g (1¾oz) chickpea (garbanzo bean) flour
2 tablespoons potato or corn starch
1 teaspoons salt
3 tablespoons extra virgin olive oil

MAIN VEG
¾ large, pointed cabbage, outer leaves removed
2 tablespoons olive oil

SAUCE
3 tablespoons sriracha sauce
3 tablespoons vegan mayo

TOPPING
2 spring onions (scallions), finely chopped
1 teaspoon finely crumbled nori (or dulse) seaweed

METHOD

PROTEIN/CARB
Tip the flour and starch and salt into a bowl or blender. Slowly pour in 2 tablespoon extra virgin olive oil and 150ml (5fl oz) water, beating with a whisk until you have a smooth, light batter (no lumps).

MAIN VEG
Slice the bottom off the cabbage so that the leaves become loose and pick 3–4 of the biggest leaves you can find (leave the rest – the core – for another recipe, see page 102). Immerse the leaves in 500ml (18fl oz) water mixed with 1 teaspoon sea salt for a few minutes (or better still, for 1 hour), then dry with a towel.

Heat the remaining olive oil in a non-stick frying pan over a medium–high heat. Dip the cabbage leaves into the batter, to lightly coat, shaking off any excess. When the oil is hot in the pan, fry the cabbage leaves (ensuring each leaf is nice and flat) for 1–2 minutes, then, using tongs, flip and cook for 1–2 minutes on the other side. Keep flipping until you reach your preferred crispiness – I like mine pretty crispy, so I cook them for a bit longer. Transfer the crispy cabbage pancakes to a plate lined with kitchen paper to soak up any excess oil and then repeat with all the leaves you have.

ASSEMBLING
Stack the pancakes on a plate, one on top of each other. Drizzle the sauces and toppings in between each layer and on top as well.

WATCH
THE ONLINE
RECIPE

POINTED CABBAGE 'SHAWARMA' WITH BUCKWHEAT & YOGURT SAUCE

INGREDIENTS

PROTEIN/CARB

1 tablespoon extra virgin olive oil
½ shallot, finely chopped
60g (2½oz) cooked buckwheat
sea salt and freshly ground black pepper

MAIN VEG

3 tablespoons olive oil
  plus extra for drizzling (optional)
3 tablespoons fresh grapefruit juice
2 garlic cloves, finely chopped
1 teaspoon onion powder
1 teaspoon ground cumin
1 teaspoon smoked paprika
1 teaspoon ground turmeric
½ teaspoon ground cinnamon
¼ teaspoon cayenne pepper
1 teaspoon sea salt
¼ teaspoon black peppercorns
½ pointed cabbage, outer leaves
  removed, then halved

SAUCE

¾ cup vegan yogurt
1 garlic clove, finely chopped or grated
2 tablespoons tahini
1 teaspoon lemon juice
sea salt, to taste

TOPPING

a sprinkle of sesame seeds
a sprinkle of fresh flat-leaf parsley

METHOD

PROTEIN/CARB

First make the sauce (see below). Heat the olive oil in a pan over a medium heat and sauté the shallot until transparent but not burned. Add the buckwheat and 2 tablespoons of the sauce and cook for a few minutes before adding 100ml (3½fl oz) water. Reduce the heat, cover the pan with a lid and simmer until the water has completely evaporated. Season with salt and pepper.

MAIN VEG

Place the olive oil, grapefruit juice, garlic and all the spices and seasonings in a resealable bag and add the cabbage halves, ensuring they are thoroughly coated. Set aside to marinate for at least 15–20 minutes (ideally overnight).

Preheat the oven to 200°C (400°F)/gas mark 6. Place the cabbage on a baking tray (sheet) lined with baking paper and cover in the marinade. Wrap the paper up tightly into a parcel and cook in the oven for 20 minutes, then uncover and baste again with the marinade to keep it moist (drizzle with more olive oil if needed). Bake for another 15–20 minutes until tender but not burned.

SAUCE

Place all the ingredients in a blender and blend until smooth.

ASSEMBLING

Spoon the sauce onto a plate, followed by the buckwheat. Arrange the cabbage on top and scatter with sesame seeds and fresh parsley.

ALTERNATIVE TIP
This recipe works very well with many different carbs, like quinoa, lentils, rice or chickpeas (garbanzo beans).

ALTERNATIVE TIP
This recipe works very well
with many different carbs,
like quinoa, lentils, rice or
beans (see page 43).

ROSTED CHINESE CABBAGE WITH BLACK RICE & MUSTARD TAHINI SAUCE

INGREDIENTS

PROTEIN/CARB

120g (4¼oz) cooked black rice
2 tablespoons olive oil
sea salt, to taste

MAIN VEG

2 tablespoons olive oil
  plus extra for drizzling (optional)
juice of ½ lemon
1 tablespoon maple syrup
1 teaspoon English mustard
½ teaspoon sea salt
½ Chinese cabbage, outer leaves
  removed, then halved

SAUCE

juice of ½ lemon
1 tablespoon maple syrup
1 teaspoon English mustard
1 teaspoon smoked paprika
2 tablespoons tahini

TOPPING

a sprinkle of fresh sprouts
a sprinkle of smoked paprika
a sprinkle of mustard seeds (optional)

METHOD

PROTEIN/CARB

Place the black rice in a bowl, stir through the olive oil and season to taste.

MAIN VEG

Place the olive oil, lemon juice, maple syrup, English mustard and salt in a resealable bag and add the cabbage halves, ensuring they are thoroughly coated. Set aside to marinate for at least 15–20 minutes (ideally overnight).

Preheat the oven to 200°C (400°F)/gas mark 6. Place the cabbage on a baking tray (sheet) lined with baking paper and cover in the marinade. Wrap the paper up tightly into a parcel and cook in the oven for 15 minutes, then uncover and baste again with the marinade to keep it moist (drizzle with more olive oil if needed). Bake for another 20–30 minutes until tender but crispy on top.

SAUCE

Place all the ingredients in a blender and blend until smooth. Check the consistency – add a little oil if the sauce is too thick.

ASSEMBLING

Spoon the rice onto a plate. Pour over half the sauce. Arrange the cabbage on top and drizzle over the remaining sauce. Scatter the sprouts, paprika and mustard seeds, if used, on top.

CHINESE CABBAGE WITH PEPPERCORNS & DILL BUTTER BEAN HUMMUS

INGREDIENTS

PROTEIN/CARB

400g (14oz) canned butter beans
2 tablespoons olive oil
 plus extra for drizzling (optional)
1 teaspoon lemon juice
a sprinkle of fresh dill
$\frac{1}{2}$ teaspoon pink peppercorns
sea salt and freshly ground
 black pepper

MAIN VEG

1 tablespoon olive oil
1 teaspoon lemon juice
1 teaspoon sea salt
1 teaspoon pink peppercorns
$\frac{1}{2}$ Chinese cabbage, outer leaves
 removed, then halved

SAUCE

1 tablespoon olive oil
juice of $\frac{1}{2}$ lemon

TOPPING

a sprinkle of fresh dill
a sprinkle of pink peppercorns
a handful of toasted pumpkin
 seeds

METHOD

PROTEIN/CARB

Strain the can of butter beans, reserving the liquid and transfer the latter to a blender. Add the oil, lemon juice, fresh dill and peppercorns and blend until smooth (add water a teaspoon at a time if necessary). Season to taste with salt and pepper.

MAIN VEG

Place the olive oil, lemon juice, salt and peppercorns in a resealable bag and add the cabbage halves, ensuring they are thoroughly coated. Set aside to marinate for at least 15–20 minutes (ideally overnight).

Preheat the oven to 200°C (400°F)/gas mark 6. Place the cabbage on a baking tray (sheet) lined with baking paper and cover in the marinade. Wrap up tightly in the baking paper and cook in the oven for 15 minutes, then uncover and baste again with the marinade to keep it moist (drizzle with more olive oil if needed). Bake for another 20–30 minutes until tender but crispy on top.

SAUCE

In a bowl, mix together the olive oil and lemon juice.

TOPPING

Spoon the dill butter bean hummus onto a plate and arrange the cabbage leaves on top. Drizzle with the sauce and scatter over the toppings.

ALTERNATIVE TIP
If you don't have a blender,
keep the beans as they are
and dress them with the
sauce ingredients.

ALTERNATIVE TIP
This recipe works very well
with many different carbs, like
quinoa, lentils, rice or beans.

MUSHROOM, ROASTED POTATOES & TRUFFLE OAT CREAM

INGREDIENTS

PROTEIN/CARB

1 large potato, peeled
1 tablespoon olive oil
a handful of fresh rosemary,
  finely chopped
sea salt and freshly ground black
  pepper, to taste

MAIN VEG

1 large portobello or white
  mushroom, de-stalked
2 garlic cloves, unpeeled
1 tablespoon olive oil
  plus extra for drizzling (optional)
a handful of fresh rosemary,
  finely chopped
1 teaspoon black peppercorns

SAUCE

2 tablespoons single (light)
  vegan cream (oat)
sea salt and freshly ground black
  pepper, to taste

TOPPING

a handful of broken walnuts
1 teaspoon truffle oil

METHOD

PROTEIN/CARB

Preheat the oven to 200°C (400°F)/gas mark 6. Cut the potato into rounds, toss with olive oil and a sprinkle of rosemary and place on a baking tray (sheet) lined with baking paper. Bake for 20–25 minutes until golden, then season to taste.

MAIN VEG

Place the mushroom and garlic on a baking tray (sheet) lined with baking paper. Drizzle with oil and sprinkle with rosemary and black peppercorns. Wrap them up tightly in the paper into a parcel and cook in the oven for 20 minutes, then uncover, remove the garlic, drizzle with more olive oil if needed and bake for a further 5–10 minutes.

SAUCE

Squeeze out the insides of the garlic cloves, which should look like a paste, and mix with the vegan cream, then season with salt and pepper to taste.

ASSEMBLING

Spoon the sauce onto a plate and place the potatoes alongside. Add the mushroom on top and scatter over the toppings.

PORTOBELLO MUSHROOM WITH ROASTED CORN & BBQ SAUCE

INGREDIENTS

PROTEIN/CARB
1 tablespoon olive oil
½ shallot, finely chopped
1 garlic clove, minced
120g (4¼oz) sweetcorn

MAIN VEG
1 tablespoon olive oil
1 large portobello or white
  mushroom, de-stalked

SAUCE
2 tablespoons ketchup
1 tablespoon tomato concentrate
1 tablespoon maple syrup
1 tablespoon brown sugar
1 tablespoon soy sauce
1 teaspoon ground ginger
1 teaspoon Worcestershire sauce
1 tablespoon olive oil

TOPPING
a sprinkle of fresh flat-leaf parsley
a sprinkle of pumpkin seeds

METHOD

PROTEIN/CARB
First make the sauce (see below). Heat the olive oil in a pan over a medium heat and sauté the shallot and garlic until transparent but not burned. Add the corn and fry gently for another 10 minutes, then add 1 tablespoon of the sauce and stir through. Take off the heat.

MAIN VEG
Heat the olive oil in a pan over a high heat and fry the mushroom for about 10–15 minutes, turning to sear both sides, until softened. Reduce the heat to medium, add 2 tablespoons of the sauce, and cook for another 10 minutes, again turning the mushroom on both sides.

SAUCE
Place all the ingredients in a blender and blend until smooth.

ASSEMBLING
Spoon the remaining sauce onto a plate and add the sweetcorn mixture, followed by the mushroom. Finish with a final drizzle of sauce and a sprinkle of parsley and pumpkin seeds.

ALTERNATIVE TIP
This recipe works very well
with many different carbs,
like quinoa, lentils, rice,
chickpeas (garbanzo bean)
or beans.

ALTERNATIVE TIP
This recipe works well with
different carbs, like potatoes,
quinoa or even buckwheat.

PORTOBELLO MUSHROOM WITH BASIL PESTO & BUTTER BEAN HUMMUS

INGREDIENTS

PROTEIN/CARB

120g (4 ¼oz) butter beans, drained
juice of ½ lemon
2 tablespoons extra virgin olive oil
1 teaspoon sea salt

MAIN VEG

1 large portobello or white mushroom,
 de-stalked
2 garlic cloves, unpeeled
1 tablespoon olive oil
 plus extra for drizzling (optional)
1 teaspoon sea salt

SAUCE

a bunch of fresh basil
3–4 tablespoons olive oil
1 teaspoon nutritional yeast
¼ teaspoon sea salt
2 tablespoons flaked almonds

TOPPING

a handful of almond flakes (better toasted)
a handful of fresh basil

METHOD

PROTEIN/CARB

First roast the mushrooms and garlic (see Main Veg, below). Squeeze out the inside of 1 roasted garlic clove, which should look like a paste, and place in a blender along with the butter beans, lemon juice, olive oil and salt. Blend until smooth.

MAIN VEG

Preheat the oven to 200°C (400°F)/gas mark 6. Place the mushroom and garlic on a baking tray (sheet) lined with baking paper and drizzle with oil and sprinkle with salt. Wrap them up tightly in the paper into a parcel and cook in the oven for 20 minutes, then uncover, remove the garlic, drizzle with more olive oil if needed and bake for a further 5–10 minutes.

SAUCE

Squeeze out the inside of the remaining garlic clove, which should look like a paste, and place in a blender along with the basil, olive oil, nutritional yeast and salt and blend until smooth, then stir through the broken nuts.

ASSEMBLING

Spoon the sauce onto a plate along with the butter bean hummus and arrange the mushroom on top. Scatter with almond flakes and fresh basil.

WATCH
THE ONLINE
RECIPE

MUSHROOM STEAK, SAFFRON OAT 'PORRIDGE'(OATMEAL) & DILL

INGREDIENTS

PROTEIN/CARB

2 tablespoons extra virgin olive oil

½ shallot, finely chopped

1 garlic clove, finely chopped

120ml (3¾fl oz) plant-based milk (rice, almond or oat)

1 teaspoon sea salt

1 teaspoon saffron

1 teaspoon porcini mushroom powder

60g (2½oz) rolled oats

2 tablespoons vegan butter

sea salt and freshly ground black pepper

MAIN VEG

1 large portobello or white mushroom, de-stalked

2 garlic cloves, unpeeled

2 bay leaves

1 tablespoon olive oil

60g (2½oz) chickpea (garbanzo bean) flour

60g (2½ cup) corn starch

½ teaspoon salt

250ml (9fl oz) sparkling water

3 tablespoons rolled oats

500ml (18fl oz) vegetable oil

TOPPING

a drizzle of extra virgin olive oil

a sprinkle of saffron

a sprinkle of fresh dill

METHOD

PROTEIN/CARB

Heat the olive oil in a pan over a medium heat and sauté the shallot and garlic gently for about 10–15 minutes until softened. Add the milk, salt, saffron and porcini mushroom powder and stir. Add the oats and butter and keep stirring for around 10 minutes. Don't let the porridge dry too much as this recipe doesn't have a sauce so add more milk and butter if necessary. Season to taste with salt and pepper.

MAIN VEG

Preheat the oven to 200°C (400°F)/gas mark 6. Place the mushrooms, garlic and bay leaves on a baking tray (sheet) lined with baking paper and drizzle with oil and sprinkle with salt. Wrap them up tightly into a parcel in the paper and cook in the oven for 20 minutes, then uncover, remove the garlic and bay leaves and prepare the batter.

Place the flour and starch in a bowl with the sea salt and whisk in the sparkling water when you are ready to use. Place the rolled oats in a shallow plate next to the batter. Pour the vegetable oil into a saucepan or deep frying pan (skillet) and, when it's hot, dip the mushroom into the batter to lightly coat, shaking off any excess, and then into the oats. Fry the mushroom steak for 2–3 minutes, then flip and cook for 1–2 minutes on the other side. When the crust is golden all over, transfer to a plate lined with kitchen paper to soak up any excess oil.

ASSEMBLING

Spoon the porridge onto a plate and place the mushroom steak on top. Finish with a drizzle of extra virgin olive oil and a scattering of toppings.

ALTERNATIVE TIP
This recipe works very well
with other carbs, like quinoa,
buckwheat, and especially
risotto rice.

ALTERNATIVE TIP

This recipe works very well with other carbs like beans, buckwheat, or even big chunky breadcrumbs (page 143) with steamed tomatoes.

PORTOBELLO MUSHROOM WITH BLACK LENTILS & TOMATO SAUCE

INGREDIENTS

PROTEIN/CARB

60g (2½oz) black lentils
1 teaspoon vegetable bouillon powder
2 tablespoons olive oil
½ teaspoon sea salt

MAIN VEG

2 tablespoons olive oil
2 tablespoons balsamic vinegar
2 garlic cloves, minced
¼ teaspoon brown sugar
a handful of fresh oregano
sea salt, to taste
½ teaspoon coarse black pepper
1 large portobello or white mushroom,
  de-stalked

SAUCE

1 tablespoon olive oil
½ shallot, finely chopped
200g (7fl oz) chopped tomatoes
1 teaspoon brown sugar
¼ teaspoon salt

TOPPING

a drizzle of extra virgin olive oil
1 tablespoon vegan hard cheeze, crumbled
a handful of fresh oregano leaves

METHOD

PROTEIN/CARB

Rinse the lentils with fresh water before cooking to remove any dust or debris. Transfer to a pan, together with 180ml (6¼fl oz) water. Stir through the vegetable bouillon powder and bring to the boil, then reduce the heat, cover tightly and simmer for 15–20 minutes until tender. Stir through the oil and salt after cooking.

MAIN VEG

Preheat the oven to 200°C (400°F)/gas mark 6. Place the olive oil, balsamic vinegar, garlic, brown sugar, oregano, salt and pepper in a bowl and mix well. Place the mushroom on a sheet of aluminium foil, cover with the marinade and wrap the foil up tightly. Place the wrapped mushroom on a baking tray (sheet) and place in the oven for 25 minutes, then uncover and bake for a further 5 minutes.

SAUCE

Heat the olive oil in a pan over a medium heat and sauté the shallot until transparent but not burned. Add the tomato, stir through the brown sugar and salt and cook for 20 minutes.

ASSEMBLING

Spoon the lentils onto a plate, followed by the tomato sauce. Arrange the mushroom steak on top. Finish with a drizzle of extra virgin olive oil and a scattering of cheeze and oregano.

FRIED OYSTER MUSHROOMS WITH JASMINE RICE & SRIRACHA SAUCE

INGREDIENTS

PROTEIN/CARB

1 tablespoon vegetable oil

½ teaspoon minced garlic

1 tablespoon kimchi

120g (4¼oz) cooked basmati rice

½ tablespoon toasted sesame oil

MAIN VEG

1 tablespoon vegetable oil

2–3 big oyster mushrooms (the biggest you can find), de-stalked

sea salt, to taste

SAUCE

2 tablespoons sriracha sauce (or another hot chilli sauce)

TOPPINGS

1 tablespoon toasted sesame seeds

1 spring onion (scallion), thinly sliced

METHOD

PROTEIN/CARB

Place a large pan or wok over a medium–high heat and, when hot, add the vegetable oil, swirling it around the pan to get hot. Add the garlic and stir-fry quickly for about 10 seconds, then add the kimchi and stir until 80 per cent of it is cooked. Reduce the heat to medium low and add the rice. Toss the pan until everything is thoroughly mixed and coated. Add the sesame oil and mix again, then set aside.

MAIN VEG

Preheat a pan over a high heat and add the oil. When the oil is nice and hot, add the mushrooms and fry on both sides until the skin is crisp but not burned. Remove from the pan and transfer to a plate lined with kitchen paper, to soak up any excess oil. Season with salt to taste.

ASSEMBLING

Spoon the rice onto a plate and lay the mushrooms on top. Drizzle with the sriracha sauce and scatter over the toppings.

WATCH
THE ONLINE
RECIPE

ALTERNATIVE TIP
If you can't find sriracha sauce,
you can make something
similar by adding 1 tablespoon
harissa paste to 2 tablespoons
ketchup – it's not the same, but
will do the job.

ALTERNATIVE TIP
If you don't fancy the chickpea (garbanzo bean) pancakes, you can replace them with other carbs, like steamed potatoes (see page 35), buckwheat pancakes (page 216) or even polenta (page 100).

FRIED OYSTER MUSHROOMS WITH CHICKPEA (GARBANZO BEAN) PANCAKES & TAHINI SAUCE

INGREDIENTS

PROTEIN/CARB

50g (2oz) chickpea
(garbanzo bean) flour

2 tablespoons potato or
corn starch

3 tablespoons extra virgin olive oil

MAIN VEG

1 tablespoon vegetable oil

a few fresh sage leaves

2–4 (depending on size) big oyster
mushrooms

sea salt, to taste

SAUCE

3½ tablespoons plant-based
milk (rice or oat work best)

1 tablespoon tahini paste

sea salt, to taste

TOPPINGS

1 tablespoon toasted sesame seeds

METHOD

PROTEIN/CARB

Tip the flour and starch into a bowl or blender. Slowly pour 2 tablespoons of oil and 150ml (5fl oz) water, beating with a whisk until you have a smooth, light batter (no lumps).

Heat the remaining tablespoon of oil in a non-stick frying pan over a medium–high heat. Pour in the batter, tilting the pan a little to ensure a thin and even layer. When the sides are crispy enough and the top is bubbly, use a spatula to gently flip the pancake and cook the other side. Keep flipping until you reach your preferred crispiness – I like it pretty crispy, so I cook it for a bit longer. You can also make smaller pancakes (like the ones in the picture) by pouring only a third of the mix into the pan at a time.

MAIN VEG

Preheat a pan over a high heat and add the oil. When the oil is nice and hot, add the sage leaves and let them crisp up for a minute or two, then remove from the pan and reserve for a topping. Add the mushrooms and fry on both sides until the skin is crisp but not burned. Remove from the pan and transfer to a plate lined with kitchen paper, to soak up any excess oil. Season with salt to taste.

SAUCE

Place all the ingredients in a blender and blend until smooth. Check the consistency – add a little more tahini until creamy enough for you.

ASSEMBLING

Spoon the sauce onto a plate, followed by the pancakes and mushrooms. Scatter with the crispy sage leaves and sesame seeds.

ROASTED RED ONION WITH BUCKWHEAT & COCONUT YOGURT

INGREDIENTS

MAIN VEG

3 tablespoons lemon juice

3 tablespoons extra virgin oil
plus extra, for drizzling

1 tablespoon maple syrup or
brown sugar

2 garlic cloves, minced

a handful of fresh thyme

1 teaspoon sea salt

1 large red onion

PROTEIN/CARB

60g (2½oz) buckwheat

1 tablespoon olive oil

a pinch of sea salt

SAUCE

2 tablespoons vegan yogurt (oat
or coconut)

TOPPING

a sprinkle of broken pistachios

a sprinkle of fresh basil

METHOD

MAIN VEG

Preheat the oven to 200°C (400°F)/gas mark 6. Place the lemon juice, oil, maple syrup or sugar, garlic, thyme and salt in a resealable bag. Slice the bottom off the onion and add to the bag, ensuring it is thoroughly coated, then set aside to marinate for 10–15 minutes.

Place the onion on a baking tray (sheet) lined with baking paper and cover in the marinade. Wrap up tightly in the paper and cook in the oven for 20 minutes, then uncover and baste again with the marinade to keep it moist (drizzle with more olive oil if needed). Bake for a further 20 minutes until tender but crispy on top.

PROTEIN/CARB

Place the buckwheat in a deep pan, cover with 120ml (3¾fl oz) water and bring to the boil. Reduce to a simmer, cover and cook until the water has evaporated completely. Strain the buckwheat through a colander and rinse under hot water to remove the starchy and foxy bits. Set aside to drain, then when it's dry, transfer to a bowl and stir through the oil and sea salt to taste.

ASSEMBLING

Spoon the buckwheat onto a plate along with the yogurt. Top with the onion and scatter over the pistachios and fresh basil.

ALTERNATIVE TIP
If you don't like buckwheat,
this recipe works well with
quinoa, rice, or even gluten-
free couscous.

ALTERNATIVE TIP
If you are not bothered about
making a béchamel, this
recipe works well with tomato
sauce (see page 56) or just a
simple oat cream.

RED ONION, ROASTED POTATOES & THYME & MUSHROOM BÉCHAMEL

INGREDIENTS

PROTEIN/CARB

1 large potato, peeled
2 teaspoons olive oil
½ teaspoon sea salt

MAIN VEG

2 tablespoons cider vinegar
3 tablespoons extra virgin olive oil
  plus extra for drizzling (optional)
1 tablespoon maple syrup or
  brown sugar
2 garlic cloves, minced
a handful of fresh thyme
1 teaspoon sea salt
1 large red onion

SAUCE

2 tablespoons olive oil
shallot, finely chopped
a handful of brown mushrooms
1 garlic clove, finely chopped
a handful of fresh thyme
100ml (3½fl oz) oat cream
1 tablespoon gluten-free flour
  (oat, buckwheat or rice)
¼ teaspoon sea salt

TOPPING

a handful of broken walnuts
a handful of fresh thyme leaves

METHOD

PROTEIN/CARB

Preheat the oven to 200°C (400°F)/gas mark 6. Spread the potato cubes out over a baking tray (sheet) lined with baking paper, drizzle with olive oil and sprinkle with salt. Bake for 30 minutes until tender, then season to taste.

MAIN VEG

Place the vinegar, oil, maple syrup or sugar, garlic, thyme and salt in a resealable bag. Slice the bottom off the onion and add to the bag, ensuring it is thoroughly coated, then set aside to marinate for 10–15 minutes.

Place the onion on a baking tray (sheet) lined with baking paper and cover in the marinade. Wrap up tightly in the paper and cook in the oven for 20 minutes, then uncover and baste again with the marinade to keep it moist (drizzle with more olive oil if needed). Bake for a further 20 minutes until tender but crispy on top.

SAUCE

Heat the olive oil in a pan over a medium heat and sauté the shallot until transparent but not burned. Add the mushrooms and garlic and cook for about 5 minutes, then stir through the thyme and oat cream. Cover with a lid and simmer for 5 minutes, then strain through a colander, reserving only the liquid. Return the liquid to the pan, sift in the flour, stir gently over a low heat until slightly thickened and completely smooth, then season to taste.

ASSEMBLING

Spoon the sauce onto a plate and tip the potato on top. Finish with the onion and a scattering of toppings.

TERIYAKI RED ONION WITH PANCAKES, AVOCADO & KIMCHI

INGREDIENTS

MAIN VEG

2 tablespoons soy sauce
1 tablespoon toasted sesame oil
2 tablespoons fresh orange juice
1 teaspoon brown sugar
2 garlic cloves, minced
1 teaspoon grated fresh ginger
1 tablespoon vegetable oil
1 large red onion

PROTEIN/CARB

50g (2oz) chickpea
   (garbanzo bean) flour
2 tablespoons potato flour or
   cornflour (corn starch)
2 tablespoons olive oil
½ small red onion, finely
   chopped
1 tablespoon vegetable oil

SAUCE

1 ripe avocado
1 tablespoon kimchi juice
1 tablespoon avocado oil
sea salt and freshly ground
   black pepper, to taste

TOPPINGS

1 tablespoon hulled hemp seeds
1 tablespoon kimchi
a handful of fresh coriander
   (cilantro) leaves

METHOD

MAIN VEG

Preheat the oven to 200°C (400°F)/gas mark 6. Place the soy sauce, sesame oil, juice, sugar, garlic, ginger and vegetable oil in a resealable bag. Slice the bottom off the onion and add to the bag, ensuring it is thoroughly coated, then set aside to marinate for 15–20 minutes.

Place the onion on a baking tray (sheet) lined with baking paper and cover in the marinade. Wrap up tightly in the paper and cook in the oven for 20 minutes, then uncover and baste again with the marinade to keep it moist (drizzle with more olive oil if needed). Bake for a further 20 minutes until tender but crispy on top.

PROTEIN/CARB

Tip the flour and starch into a bowl or blender. Slowly pour in the olive oil and 150ml (5fl oz) water, beating with a whisk until you have a smooth, light batter (no lumps). Add the red onion and mix well.

Heat the vegetable oil in a non-stick frying pan over a medium–high heat. Pour in the batter, tilting the pan a little to ensure a thin and even layer. When the sides are crispy enough and the top is bubbly, use a spatula to gently flip the pancake and cook the other side. Keep flipping until you reach your preferred crispiness – I like it pretty crispy, so I cook it for a bit longer. You can also make smaller pancakes (like the ones in the picture) by pouring only a third of the mix into the pan at a time.

SAUCE

Place all the ingredients in a blender and blend until smooth. Check the consistency – if too thin, just add a little extra oil until creamy enough for you.

ASSEMBLING

Spoon the sauce onto a plate and layer with the pancakes and then the onion. Finish with the toppings and serve.

ALTERNATIVE TIP
If you don't fancy the
chickpea (garbanzo bean)
pancakes, you can replace it
with other carbs like white
rice, black beans or
crispy potatoes.

ALTERNATIVE TIP
Swap the cream with a more
hot and spicy sauce from
page 124.

ROASTED RED ONION IN AN OREGANO & WHITE WINE CREAM

INGREDIENTS

PROTEIN/CARB

60g (2½oz) gluten-free bread, broken
  into chunks
2 garlic cloves, finely chopped
1 tablespoon olive oil

MAIN VEG

2 tablespoons white wine
3 tablespoons extra virgin olive oil
  plus extra for drizzling (
1 tablespoon maple syrup or
  brown sugar
2 garlic cloves, minced
a handful of fresh oregano
1 teaspoon sea salt
1 big red onion

SAUCE

2 tablespoons olive oil
½ small white onion, finely chopped
1 garlic clove, minced
a handful of fresh oregano
2 tablespoons white wine
100ml (3½fl oz) vegetable stock (broth)
1 tablespoon gluten-free flour of your
  choice (oat, buckwheat or rice)
sea salt and freshly ground
  black pepper, to taste

TOPPINGS

1 tablespoon hard vegan cheeze, grated
a handful of fresh oregano leaves

METHOD

MAIN VEG

Preheat the oven to 200°C (400°F)/gas mark 6. Place the wine, oil, maple syrup or sugar, garlic, oregano and salt in a resealable bag. Slice the bottom off the onion and add to the bag, ensuring it is thoroughly coated, then set aside to marinate for 10–15 minutes.

Place the onion on a baking tray (sheet) lined with baking paper and cover in the marinade. Wrap up tightly in the paper and cook in the oven for 40 minutes, then uncover and baste again with the marinade to keep it moist (drizzle with more olive oil if needed). Bake for a further 15 minutes until tender but crispy on top.

PROTEIN/CARB

Place the bread chunks in a roasting tin and toss with the garlic and oil. Bake in the oven for 10 minutes.

SAUCE

Heat the olive oil in a pan over a medium heat and sauté the onion and garlic until transparent but not burned. Add the oregano and white wine and cook, letting the alcohol evaporate, then pour in the stock (broth), cover with a lid and simmer for 5 minutes. Strain through a colander, reserving only the liquid. Return the liquid to the pan, sift in the flour and stir gently over a low heat until slightly thickened and completely smooth.

ASSEMBLING

Spoon the sauce onto a plate and scatter over the crispy croutons. Arrange the onion on top and scatter over the cheeze and oregano.

CARAMELIZED WHITE ONION WITH KIDNEY BEANS & RED (BELL) PEPPER SAUCE

INGREDIENTS

PROTEIN/CARB

120g (4¼oz) cooked kidney beans
1 tablespoon olive oil

MAIN VEG

3 tablespoons extra virgin
  olive oil plus extra, for
  drizzling (optional)
2 tablespoons maple syrup or
  brown sugar
1 teaspoon apple cider vinegar
1 teaspoon sea salt
1 big white onion

SAUCE

1 large red (bell) pepper, deseeded
  and chopped
1 tablespoon olive oil
½ shallot, finely chopped
2 garlic cloves, finely chopped
2 tablespoons tomato salsa sauce
¼ teaspoon salt

TOPPING

1 tablespoon olive oil
a handful of fresh flat-leaf parsley
1 teaspoon hulled hemp seeds
sea salt and freshly ground
  black pepper, to taste

METHOD

MAIN VEG

Preheat the oven to 200°C (400°F)/gas mark 6. Place the oil, maple syrup and sugar, vinegar and salt in a resealable bag. Slice the bottom off the onion and add to the bag, ensuring it is thoroughly coated, then set aside to marinate for 10–15 minutes.

Place the onion on a baking tray (sheet) lined with baking paper and cover in the marinade. Wrap up tightly in the paper and cook in the oven for 40 minutes, then uncover and baste again with the marinade to keep it moist (drizzle with more olive oil if needed). Bake for a further 15 minutes until tender but crispy on top.

SAUCE

Place the pepper in a roasting tin, drizzle with 1 tablespoon of olive oil and roast in the oven for 30 minutes. Heat the remaining olive oil in a pan over a medium heat and sauté the shallot and garlic until transparent but not burned. Add the tomato salsa sauce, salt and roasted red pepper, then cover with a lid and simmer for 10 minutes.

ASSEMBLING

Stir the sauce through the beans with a tablespoon of olive oil and spoon onto a plate. Arrange the onion on top, scatter with parsley and hemp seeds and season to taste.

ALTERNATIVE TIP
Swap the pepper sauce with
the milder tahini sauce from
page 119.

ALTERNATIVE TIP
If you don't want to use
quinoa, you can use many
different carbs like buckwheat,
rice or even pancakes.

ROASTED WHITE ONION WITH RED QUINOA & LEMON & MUSTARD TAHINI CREAM

INGREDIENTS

PROTEIN/CARB
120g (4¼oz) cooked red quinoa

MAIN VEG
1 big white onion
2 tablespoons olive oil
2 tablespoons lemon juice
1 tablespoon brown sugar
1 tablespoon tamari soy sauce
2 garlic cloves, minced
⅓ teaspoon sea salt
¼ teaspoon black pepper

SAUCE
1 tablespoon tahini
3½ tablespoons plant-based milk
   (rice or oat work best)
1 teaspoon English mustard
sea salt, to taste

TOPPING
2 teaspoons lemon zest
1 teaspoon pine nuts, toasted if liked
a handful of pink peppercorns

METHOD

MAIN VEG
Place the oil, lemon juice, sugar, soy sauce, garlic, salt and pepper in a resealable bag, reserving 1 tablespoon of oil for later, and add the onion, ensuring it is thoroughly coated, then set aside to marinate for 10–15 minutes.

Preheat the oven to 200°C (400°F)/gas mark 6. Remove the onion from the marinade and place on a baking tray (sheet) lined with baking paper, drizzle with the remaining oil, sprinkle with salt and place in the oven for 40 minutes. Remove from the oven, pour the marinade on top of the onion and bake for a further 15 minutes, until tender but a little crispy on top.

SAUCE
Place all the ingredients in a blender and blend until smooth. Check the consistency – add a little tahini until creamy.

ASSEMBLING
Spoon the sauce onto a plate and layer with the quinoa. Place the onion on top and open to create the same 'flower' effect (see image). Finish with a scattering of lemon thyme, pine nuts and pink peppercorns.

CANDY BEETROOT (BEET) 'BRESAOLA' WITH PARSLEY PESTO & CHICKPEA HUMMUS

INGREDIENTS

PROTEIN/CARB

120g (4¼oz) cooked chickpeas
2 tablespoons olive oil
¼ teaspoon sea salt

MAIN VEG

1 large candy beetroot (beet), topped
  and tailed
1 tablespoon extra virgin olive oil
sea salt and freshly ground
  black pepper, to taste

SAUCE

a bunch of fresh flat-leaf parsley
1 teaspoon lemon juice
4 tablespoons olive oil
¼ teaspoon sea salt
1 teaspoon nutritional yeast
2 tablespoons almond flakes

TOPPING

a sprinkle of almond flakes
2 sun-dried tomatoes, finely chopped

METHOD

PROTEIN/CARB

Place the ingredients in a blender with 1 tablespoon water and blend until smooth.

MAIN VEG

Preheat the oven to 200°C (400°F)/gas mark 6. Slice the beetroot very thinly and arrange on a baking tray (sheet) lined with baking paper. Drizzle with oil and sprinkle with salt and pepper and bake for 35–45 minutes until tender.

SAUCE

Place the parsley, lemon juice, olive oil, salt, nutritional yeast and half the almond flakes in a blender and blend until smooth, then stir through the remaining almond flakes.

ASSEMBLING

Spoon the sauce onto a plate with the hummus. Arrange the beetroot slices on top and scatter over the toppings.

ALTERNATIVE TIP
If you don't have the time
to make the hummus, you
can buy it, and same for
the pesto.

ALTERNATIVE TIP
If you don't have butter
beans, this recipe works well
with other carbs too, like
bread chunks (see page 27),
lentils or even quinoa.

ROASTED CANDY BEETROOT (BEET) WITH OLIVES, CAPERS & TOMATO BEANS

INGREDIENTS

PROTEIN/CARB
120g (4¼oz) cooked butter beans

MAIN VEG
1 large candy beetroot (beet),
  quartered
1 tablespoon extra virgin olive oil
1 teaspoon sea salt

SAUCE
1 tablespoon olive oil
½ shallot, finely chopped
200g (fl oz) chopped tomatoes
1 teaspoon brown sugar
¼ teaspoon salt

TOPPING
1 tablespoon capers
1 tablespoon pitted and chopped
  black olives
a handful of fresh parsley
sea salt and freshly ground
  black pepper, to taste

METHOD

MAIN VEG
Preheat the oven to 200°C (400°F)/gas mark 6. Arrange the beetroot on a baking tray (sheet) lined with baking paper, drizzle with oil, sprinkle with salt and toss to coat evenly. Bake for 1 hour until tender.

SAUCE
Heat the olive oil in a pan over a medium heat and sauté the shallot until transparent but not burned. Add the tomato, sugar and salt, then cover with a lid and simmer for 20 minutes.

ASSEMBLING
Stir the beans into the sauce along with a little of the toppings. Arrange the beetroot chunks on top and scatter with the remaining toppings. Season to taste with salt and pepper.

BEETROOT (BEET), CHICKPEA (GARBANZO BEAN) PANCAKES & TAHINI & MUSTARD SAUCE

INGREDIENTS

MAIN VEG

3 tablespoons extra virgin olive oil
  plus extra for drizzling
2 tablespoons cider vinegar
1 tablespoon English mustard
1 tablespoon maple syrup
a handful of mustard seeds
1 tablespoon sea salt
1 teaspoon coarse black peppercorns
1 large candy beetroot (beet)

PROTEIN/CARB

50g (2¼oz) chickpea
  (garbanzo bean) flour
2 tablespoons potato or corn starch
3 tablespoons extra virgin olive oil
1 tablespoon smoked paprika
1 teaspoon garlic powder

SAUCE

1 tablespoon tahini
3½ tablespoons plant-based milk
1 tablespoon vegan mayo
1 teaspoon English mustard
1 teaspoon maple syrup or rice syrup
½ teaspoon salt

TOPPING

a sprinkle of toasted mustard seeds
a handful of fresh flat-leaf parsley
1 tablespoon small gherkin (pickle),
  sliced
sea salt and freshly ground black
  pepper, to taste

METHOD

MAIN VEG

Preheat the oven to 200°C (400°F)/gas mark 6. Place all the ingredients except the beetroot in a resealable bag and add the beetroot, ensuring it is thoroughly coated, then set aside to marinate for at least 10–15 minutes (or ideally overnight).

Remove the beetroot from the marinade and place on a baking tray (sheet) lined with baking paper, drizzle with oil, sprinkle with salt and place in the oven for 40 minutes. Remove from the oven, pour the marinade on top of the beetroot. Bake for a further 15 minutes until completely tender. Discard the marinade and, with a sharp knife, thinly slice the beetroot.

PROTEIN/CARB

Tip the flour and starch into a bowl or blender. Slowly pour in 2 tablespoons oil and 150ml (5fl oz) water, reserving 1 tablespoon of oil for later. Beat with a whisk until you have a smooth, light batter (no lumps). Sprinkle in smoked paprika and garlic powder and mix well.

Heat the remaining oil in a non-stick frying pan over a medium–high heat. Pour in the batter, tilting the pan a little to ensure a thin and even layer. When the sides are crispy and the top is bubbly, gently flip the pancake and cook the other side. For smaller pancakes (like in the picture), pour half the mix into the pan at a time.

SAUCE

Place all the ingredients in a blender and blend until smooth. Check the consistency – add a little tahini until creamy enough for you.

ASSEMBLING

Spoon the sauce onto a plate and add the pancakes. Lay the beetroot slices on top, scatter over the toppings and season to taste.

ALTERNATIVE TIP
Swap the creamy sauce for the
hot and spicy one on page 204.

ALTERNATIVE TIP

If you are not keen on lentils, this recipe works well also with other carbs like quinoa, buckwheat or roasted (broiled) potatoes.

GARLIC & OREGANO-BAKED BEETROOT (BEET) WITH VEGAN CHEEZE & BROWN LENTILS

INGREDIENTS

MAIN VEG

1 large beetroot (beet), topped
  and tailed
3 tablespoons extra virgin olive oil
a handful of fresh oregano
2 garlic cloves, finely chopped
1 teaspoon sea salt
1 teaspoon coarse black peppercorns

PROTEIN/CARB

60g (2½oz) brown lentils
1 shallot, finely chopped
1 teaspoon vegetable bouillon
  powder (stock)
2 tablespoons olive oil
½ teaspoon sea salt

TOPPING

2 tablespoons grated vegan
  hard cheeze
1 teaspoon fresh oregano leaves
1 teaspoon almond flakes
sea salt and freshly ground black
  pepper, to taste

METHOD

MAIN VEG

Place the oil (reserving 1 teaspoon for later), oregano, garlic, salt and peppercorns in a resealable bag and add the beetroot, ensuring it is thoroughly coated, then set aside to marinate for at least 10–15 minutes (or ideally overnight).

Preheat the oven to 200°C (400°F)/gas mark 6. Remove the beetroot from the marinade and place on a baking tray (sheet) lined with baking paper, drizzle with oil, sprinkle with salt and place in the oven for 40 minutes. Remove from the oven, pour the marinade on top of the beetroot and bake for a further 15 minutes until completely tender.

PROTEIN/CARB

Rinse the lentils with fresh water before cooking to remove any dust or debris. Heat the oil in a heavy-bottomed pan over a medium heat and sauté the shallot for about 5 minutes, being careful not to burn it. Add the lentils and 180ml (6¼fl oz) water and stir through the stock (broth) powder. Bring to the boil, cover tightly, reduce the heat and simmer until the lentils are tender (15–20 minutes). Stir through the oil and salt after cooking. This recipe doesn't have a sauce as it relies on the creaminess of the cheeze and lentils, so make sure they are not too dry.

ASSEMBLING

Spoon the lentils onto a plate and place the beetroot on top. Scatter over all the toppings and season to taste.

SALT & THYME BEETROOT (BEET) WITH BUCKWHEAT & LEMON BÉCHAMEL

INGREDIENTS

MAIN VEG

3 tablespoons extra virgin olive oil
a handful of fresh lemon thyme
1 tablespoon sea salt
1 large beetroot (beet),
  topped and tailed

PROTEIN/CARB

60g (2½oz) buckwheat
1 tablespoon olive oil
a pinch of sea salt

SAUCE

½ shallot
2 tablespoons olive oil
1 garlic clove, finely chopped
1 tablespoon lemon juice
100ml (3½fl oz) plant-based milk
  (oat or rice)
1 tablespoon gluten-free flour of
  your choice (oat, buckwheat or rice)

TOPPING

1 teaspoon fresh lemon thyme leaves
1 teaspoon grated lemon zest
sea salt and freshly ground black
  pepper, to taste

METHOD

MAIN VEG

Place the oil, lemon thyme and salt in a resealable bag and add the beetroot, ensuring it is thoroughly coated, then set aside to marinate for at least 10–15 minutes (or ideally overnight).

Preheat the oven to 200°C (400°F)/gas mark 6. Remove the beetroot from the marinade and place on a baking tray (sheet) lined with baking paper, drizzle with oil, sprinkle with salt and place in the oven for 40 minutes. Remove from the oven, pour the marinade on top of the beetroot and bake for a further 15 minutes until completely tender.

PROTEIN/CARB

Place the buckwheat in a deep pan, cover with 120ml (3¾fl oz) water and bring to the boil. Reduce to a simmer, cover and cook until the water has evaporated completely. Strain the buckwheat through a colander and rinse under hot water to remove the starchy and foxy bits. Set aside to drain, then when it's dry, transfer to a bowl and stir through the oil and sea salt to taste.

SAUCE

Place the shallot and garlic with the olive oil in a blender and blend to a purée, then transfer to a pan over medium heat and sauté for about 5 minutes, being careful not to let it burn. Stir through the lemon juice and milk, cover with a lid and simmer for 5 minutes. Sift in the flour and stir gently over a low heat until slightly thickened and completely smooth.

ASSEMBLING

Spoon the buckwheat onto a plate. Place the beetroot on top, drizzle with the sauce, scatter over the toppings and season to taste.

ALTERNATIVE TIP
If you are not keen on
buckwheat, this recipe works
well also with other carbs, like
beans, rice or steamed potatoes.

ALTERNATIVE TIP
If you don't like broad beans,
you can swap for many other
legumes like cannellini beans,
lentils or yellow split peas.

BAKED BEETROOT (BEET) WITH BROAD (FAVA) BEANS & CASHEW CREAM

INGREDIENTS

PROTEIN/CARB
120g (4¹/₄oz) podded broad
  (fava) beans
2 tablespoons olive oil
¹/₄ teaspoon sea salt

MAIN VEG
1 large beetroot (beet) or 2 small ones,
  topped and tailed
1 tablespoon extra virgin olive oil
sea salt, to taste

SAUCE
100g (3¹/₂oz) cashew nuts, soaked
1 teaspoon nutritional yeast
1 tablespoon tamari soy sauce

TOPPING
a sprinkle of fresh oregano leaves
a sprinkle of broken cashew nuts
sea salt and freshly ground black
  pepper, to taste

METHOD

PROTEIN/CARB
Place the podded beans in a pan of boiling water and cook for 2 minutes. Drain and cover with cold water to cool, then drain again and peel off the outer skins. Place the oil in a pan over a medium heat pot and sauté the beans for about 5 minutes. After, add the salt.

MAIN VEG
Preheat the oven to 200°C (400°F)/gas mark 6. Slice the beetroot very thinly and arrange on a baking tray (sheet) lined with baking paper. Drizzle with oil and sprinkle with salt and bake for 35 minutes until tender.

SAUCE
Place the ingredients in a blender with 100ml (3¹/₂fl oz) water and blend until smooth.

ASSEMBLING
Spoon the sauce onto a plate and scatter over the beans. Arrange the beetroot slices on top and sprinkle over the toppings.

ROASTED CARROTS WITH SMOKED PAPRIKA & MUSTARD YOGURT SAUCE

INGREDIENTS

MAIN VEG

2 large carrots, topped and tailed
2 tablespoons coconut oil,
  plus extra for drizzling (optional)
2 tablespoons sea salt

PROTEIN/CARB

50g (2oz) quinoa
1 tablespoon smoked paprika
1 teaspoon garlic powder
1 tablespoon olive oil - not used
a pinch of sea salt - not used

SAUCE

2 tablespoons vegan yogurt
1 tablespoon extra virgin olive oil
¼ teaspoon sea salt
1 teaspoon Dijon mustard

TOPPING

a spoonful of classic sauerkraut
a handful of fresh dill
a sprinkle of smoked paprika
a sprinkle of poppy seeds

METHOD

MAIN VEG

Preheat the oven to 200°C (400°F)/gas mark 6. Place the carrots on a baking tray (sheet) lined with baking paper, toss in the oil and salt and then fold the baking paper over to create a parcel. Place in the oven for 45 minutes, then remove from the oven, uncover and spoon the oil back over the veg to keep it wet (drizzle with more oil if needed). Bake for a further 15 minutes until completely tender.

PROTEIN/CARB

Place the quinoa in a sieve and rinse under cold running water to remove the soapy coating and any bitter flavour. Transfer the quinoa to a saucepan, cover with 100ml (3½fl oz) water, stir through the paprika and garlic powder and bring to the boil. Reduce the heat, cover with a lid and simmer for 15–20 minutes. Stir in the oil and season with salt.

SAUCE

Place the ingredients in a blender and blend until smooth.

ASSEMBLING

Spoon the sauce onto a plate, followed by the quinoa. Lay the carrots on top with a garnish of sauerkraut and scatter over the dill, poppy seeds and smoked paprika.

ALTERNATIVE TIP
If you don't like quinoa,
you can use other carbs, like
lentils, buckwheat or roasted
(broiled) potatoes.

ALTERNATIVE TIP
If you don't have rice, you
can use other grains, like
quinoa, oats or buckwheat.

ROASTED CARROT WITH RICE & SWEET TAMARI SAUCE

INGREDIENTS

SAUCE/MARINADE

3 tablespoons olive oil

3 teaspoons tamari soy sauce

1 tablespoon mirin vinegar
  or grapefruit juice

1 tablespoon maple syrup

1 garlic clove, minced

1 teaspoon toasted sesame oil

PROTEIN/CARB

100g (3½oz) cooked white rice

MAIN VEG

2 large carrots, topped and tailed

1 tablespoon olive oil

¼ teaspoon of sea salt

TOPPING

½ spring onion (scallion),
  finely chopped

a sprinkle of toasted nori flakes

a sprinkle of grated horseradish

METHOD

SAUCE

Place all the ingredients in a blender and blend until smooth.

MAIN VEG

Place all the sauce/marinade ingredients in a resealable bag, and add the carrots, ensuring they are thoroughly coated. Marinate for at least 10–15 minutes (or ideally overnight).

Preheat the oven to 200°C (400°F)/gas mark 6. Remove the carrots from the marinade and place on a baking tray (sheet) lined with baking paper, drizzle with oil, sprinkle with salt and place in the oven for 40 minutes. Remove from the oven, spoon 2 tablespoons of the marinade over the veg and bake for a further 15 minutes until completely tender. Remove the carrots, slice thinly lengthways, and spoon over some more sauce/marinade.

ASSEMBLING

Spoon the rice onto a plate and pour over the remaining sauce. Lay the carrot slices on top and scatter over the toppings.

SMOKED CARROT 'BACON' WITH CHICKPEA (GARBANZO BEAN) SCRAMBLE & AVOCADO SAUCE

INGREDIENTS

MAIN VEG
2 tablespoons olive oil
1 teaspoon tamari soy sauce
2 tablespoons smoked paprika
1 teaspoon maple syrup
1 teaspoon salt
2 large carrots, topped and tailed

PROTEIN/CARB
50g (2oz) chickpea
  (garbanzo bean) flour
1 tablespoon potato or corn starch
2 tablespoons extra virgin olive oil
1 tablespoon extra virgin olive oil
2 brown mushrooms, very
  finely chopped

SAUCE
2 tablespoons olive oil
½ shallot
1 ripe avocado
1 tablespoon lemon juice
1 teaspoon sea salt

TOPPING
a handful of fresh flat-leaf parsley
a sprinkle of toasted coconut

METHOD

MAIN VEG
Place the olive oil, tamari, paprika, maple syrup and salt in a resealable bag and add the carrots, ensuring they are thoroughly coated, then set aside to marinate for at least 10–15 minutes (or ideally overnight).

Preheat the oven to 200°C (400°F)/gas mark 6. Remove the carrots from the marinade and slice thinly lengthways into 'rashers'. Place on a baking tray (sheet) lined with baking paper, drizzle with oil, sprinkle with salt and place in the oven for 40 minutes. Remove from the oven, heat up a pan on medium high heat. Pour the marinade and one extra teaspoon of extra virgin of olive oil on top of the veg and fry for a further 10/15 minutes until slightly crispy on the outside

PROTEIN/CARB
Tip the flour and starch into a bowl or blender. Slowly pour in the oil and 150ml (5fl oz) water, beating with a whisk until you have a smooth, light batter (no lumps).

Heat 1 tablespoon oil in a non-stick frying pan over a high heat and fry the mushrooms until softened. Add more oil and, when hot, pour in the batter, tilting the pan a little to ensure a thin and even layer. Reduce the heat to medium and cook for a minute, then stir the batter, as if you were making a scramble, until it firms up into crispy chunks. I like it pretty crispy, so I cook it for at least 10–15 minutes.

SAUCE
Place all the ingredients in a blender and blend until smooth.

ASSEMBLING
Spoon the sauce onto a plate, top with the crispy chickpea scramble and then the carrot 'bacon'. Scatter over the toppings and serve.

ALTERNATIVE TIP
If you don't like the chickpea
(garbanzo bean) scramble,
you can use red lentil flour,
yellow pea flour or even
buckwheat flour.

ALTERNATIVE TIP
If you don't want to make
the buckwheat pancakes,
you can use roasted potatoes,
buckwheat or rice.

CUMIN-ROASTED CARROT WITH CHARCOAL BUCKWHEAT PANCAKES & TARRAGON YOGURT

INGREDIENTS

MAIN VEG
3 tablespoons olive oil
1 teaspoon cider vinegar
½ teaspoon sea salt
a sprig of fresh rosemary
1 teaspoon cumin seeds
freshly ground black pepper
2 large carrots, topped and tailed

PROTEIN/CARB
60g (2½oz) buckwheat flour
2 tablespoons extra virgin olive oil
1 teaspoon activated charcoal
1 teaspoon sea salt
a handful of fresh tarragon leaves

SAUCE
3 tablespoons vegan yogurt
1 teaspoon lemon juice
½ garlic clove, minced
1 tablespoon fresh tarragon
sea salt, to taste

TOPPING
a sprinkle of fresh tarragon
1 teaspoon toasted pumpkin seeds

METHOD

MAIN VEG
Place 2 tablespoons of oil (reserving 1 tablespoon of oil for late), vinegar, salt, rosemary, cumin and some pepper in a resealable bag and add the carrots, ensuring they are coated, then set aside to marinate for at least 10–15 minutes (or ideally overnight).

Preheat the oven to 200°C (400°F)/gas mark 6. Remove the carrots from the marinade and place on a baking tray (sheet) lined with baking paper, drizzle with the remaining oil, sprinkle with salt and place in the oven for 40 minutes. Remove from the oven, pour 2 tablespoons of the marinade on top and bake for a further 15 minutes until tender.

PROTEIN/CARB
Tip the flour into a bowl or blender. Slowly pour in 1 tablespoon of oil (reserving the rest for later), 150ml (5fl oz) water, 1 teaspoon of activated charcoal, 1 teaspoon sea salt. Beat with a whisk until you have a smooth, light batter (no lumps). Add the tarragon leaves and mix well.

Heat the remaining oil in a non-stick frying pan over a medium–high heat. Pour in the batter, tilting the pan a little to ensure an even layer. When the sides are crispy enough and the top is bubbly, use a spatula to gently flip the pancake and cook the other side. Keep flipping until you reach your preferred crispiness. You can also make smaller pancakes (like in the picture) by pouring only half the mix into the pan at a time.

SAUCE
Place all the ingredients in a blender and blend until smooth.

ASSEMBLING
Lay the buckwheat pancakes on a plate, spoon over the sauce, arrange the carrots on top and sprinkle over the toppings.

ALTERNATIVE TIP

If you don't like to use potatoes, you can use other carbs like beans, bread chunks or chickpeas (garbanzo beans).

MAPLE-ROASTED CARROT WITH STEAMED POTATOES & PEA CREAM

INGREDIENTS

MAIN VEG

2 tablespoons vegetable oil

1 teaspoon salt

1 teaspoon maple syrup

1 teaspoon cider vinegar

1 teaspoon English mustard

1 teaspoon dried oregano

1 garlic clove, minced

2 large carrots, topped and tailed

PROTEIN/CARB

1 large potato, peeled and
  chopped into 2.5cm (1in) cubes

SAUCE

60g (2½oz) frozen green peas

3½ tablespoons single
  (light) vegan cream

1 tablespoon olive oil

½ teaspoon sea salt

TOPPING

a handful of fresh lemon thyme

a sprinkle of pumpkin seeds

sea salt and freshly ground black
  pepper, to taste

METHOD

MAIN VEG

Place 1 tablespoon of vegetable oil (reserving the rest for later), salt, maple syrup, cider vinegar, mustard, oregano and garlic in a resealable bag and add the carrots, ensuring they are thoroughly coated, then set aside to marinate for at least 10–15 minutes (or ideally overnight).

Preheat the oven to 200°C (400°F)/gas mark 6. Remove the carrots from the marinade and place on a baking tray (sheet) lined with baking paper, drizzle with the remaining oil, sprinkle with salt and place in the oven for 40 minutes. Remove from the oven, pour the marinade on top of the veg and bake for a further 15 minutes until completely tender.

PROTEIN/CARB

Steam the potato for 15 minutes until soft but not crumbly.

SAUCE

Defrost the peas by steaming them for 4–5 minutes. Then place all the ingredients in a blender and blend until smooth.

ASSEMBLING

Spoon the sauce onto a plate and scatter over the potatoes. Lay the carrots on top and finish with the toppings.

CARAMELIZED PARSNIP WITH MUSHROOMS & QUINOA

INGREDIENTS

PROTEIN/CARB
50g (2oz) quinoa

MAIN VEG
1 teaspoon tamari soy sauce
1 teaspoon brown sugar
1 tablespoon olive oil
 plus extra, for drizzling (optional)
1 large parsnip

SAUCE
1 tablespoon olive oil
1 onion, finely chopped
fresh thyme leaves
a handful of white button mushrooms,
 finely chopped
100ml (3½fl oz) vegetable stock (broth)
1 tablespoon flour
sea salt and freshly ground
 black pepper, to taste

TOPPING
olive oil, for drizzling
a sprinkle of fresh thyme leaves
freshly ground black pepper

METHOD

PROTEIN/CARB
Preheat the oven to 200°C (400°F)/gas mark 6. Place the quinoa in a small but deep roasting tin and pour over 100ml (3½fl oz) water. Cover with baking paper and place in the oven for 10 minutes, then uncover and cook for a further 10–15 minutes.

MAIN VEG
Place the tamari, sugar and oil in a resealable bag and add the parsnip, ensuring it is thoroughly coated, then set aside to marinate for at least 15–20 minutes (or ideally overnight).

Preheat the oven to 200°C (400°F)/gas mark 6, if marinated overnight. Remove the parsnip from the marinade and place on a baking tray (sheet) lined with baking paper. Wrap the baking paper around it in a parcel and cook in the oven for 15 minutes, then unwrap, pour over the marinade (drizzle with more oil if necessary) and bake for a further 20–30 minutes until the parsnip is tender.

SAUCE
Heat the olive oil in a pan over a medium heat and sauté the onion and thyme until golden. Add the mushrooms and cook until their liquid has evaporated, then season with salt and pepper. Stir half the mixture into the cooked quinoa, then add the stock (broth) to the remaining veg in the pan and bring to the boil. Using a stick blender, blend the mixture, then sift in the flour and stir for a few minutes until slightly thickened but completely smooth.

ASSEMBLING
Spoon the quinoa mixture onto a plate, top with the parsnip, pour over the sauce, drizzle with olive oil, season with pepper and sprinkle with fresh thyme leaves.

ALTERNATIVE TIP
You can replace the quinoa
with brown rice, buckwheat
or even polenta.

ALTERNATIVE TIP

If you don't want to use rice, you can use carbs like quinoa, buckwheat or chickpea (garbanzo bean) pancakes.

TAMARI PARSNIP WITH JASMINE RICE & MISO AVOCADO SAUCE

INGREDIENTS

MAIN VEG

1 large parsnip or 2 smaller ones,
  topped and tailed
2 tablespoons soy sauce
1 tablespoon toasted sesame oil
2 tablespoons fresh orange juice
1 teaspoon brown sugar
2 garlic cloves, minced
1 teaspoon grated fresh ginger
2 tablespoon vegetable oil

PROTEIN/CARB

60g (2½oz) white basmati rice
1 tablespoon extra virgin olive oil
1 teaspoon salt

SAUCE

1 ripe avocado
1 tablespoon white miso
2 tablespoons avocado or extra
  virgin olive oil
sea salt and freshly ground black
  pepper, to taste

TOPPINGS

1 teaspoon seaweed flakes (nori
  or dulse)
1 spring onion (scallion),
  finely chopped

METHOD

MAIN VEG

Using a sharp knife, score the parsnip diagonally down each side (see image). Place the soy sauce, sesame oil, orange juice, sugar, garlic, ginger and 1 tablespoon of vegetable oil (reserving the rest for later) in a resealable bag. Then add the parsnip, ensuring it is thoroughly coated. Set aside to marinate for at least 15–20 minutes (or ideally overnight).

Preheat the oven to 200°C (400°F)/gas mark 6. Remove the parsnip from the marinade and place on a baking tray (sheet) lined with baking paper, drizzle with the remaining oil, sprinkle with salt and place in the oven for 50 minutes. Remove from the oven, pour the marinade on top of the veg and bake for a further 15 minutes until completely tender.

PROTEIN/CARB

Place the rice in a saucepan and cover with 120ml (3¾fl oz) water. Stir through the oil and salt and bring to the boil. Reduce the heat, cover with a lid, and simmer for 15–20 minutes.

SAUCE

Place all the ingredients in a blender and blend until smooth. Check the consistency – add a little more oil until creamy enough for you.

ASSEMBLING

Spoon the sauce onto a plate with the rice, lay the parsnip on top and scatter over the toppings.

ROASTED PARSNIP WITH ADUKI BEANS & SMOKED TOMATO SAUCE

INGREDIENTS

SAUCE

1 tablespoon olive oil
½ shallot, finely chopped
1 garlic clove, minced
200g (7fl oz) chopped tomatoes
2 tablespoons smoked paprika
1 teaspoon brown sugar
½ teaspoon salt

PROTEIN/CARB

120g (4¼oz) cooked aduki beans

MAIN VEG

2 tablespoons extra virgin olive oil
1 tablespoon smoked paprika
1 teaspoon maple syrup
1 teaspoon cider vinegar
1 teaspoon salt
1 large parsnip or 2 smaller ones,
  topped and tailed

TOPPING

a sprinkle of ground shelled
  hemp seeds (optional)
a sprinkle of fresh oregano

METHOD

SAUCE

Heat the olive oil in a pan over a medium heat and sauté the shallot and garlic until transparent but not burned. Add the tomato, paprika, sugar and salt, then cover with a lid and simmer for 30 minutes. Finally, turn off the heat, stir through the beans and set aside, covered, for the beans to warm through.

MAIN VEG

Using a sharp knife, deeply score the parsnip horizontally down one side (see image). Place 1 tablespoon of the olive oil (reserving the rest for later), paprika, maple syrup, cider vinegar and salt along with 2 tablespoons of the sauce in a resealable bag and add the parsnip, ensuring it is thoroughly coated, then set aside to marinate for at least 15–20 minutes (or ideally overnight).

Preheat the oven to 200°C (400°F)/gas mark 6. Remove the parsnip from the marinade and place on a baking tray (sheet) lined with baking paper, drizzle with the remaining oil, sprinkle with salt and place in the oven for 50 minutes. Remove from the oven, pour the marinade on top of the veg and bake for a further 15 minutes until completely tender.

ASSEMBLING

Spoon the beans onto a plate and lay the parsnip on top, then scatter over the toppings.

ALTERNATIVE TIP
If you don't want to use
aduki beans, you can use
other pulses like butter beans,
chickpeas (garbanzo beans)
and lentils.

ALTERNATIVE TIP
If you don't want to use
black rice, you can use other
grains or pulses like quinoa,
buckwheat or lentils.

ROASTED BUTTERNUT SQUASH WITH BLACK RICE & WALNUT CREAM

INGREDIENTS

MAIN VEG

1 large butternut squash,
  scrubbed to remove the wax
2 tablespoons extra virgin olive oil
1 teaspoon sea salt
a bunch of fresh oregano

PROTEIN/CARB

1 tablespoon extra virgin olive oil
½ shallot, finely chopped
120g (4¼oz) cooked black beans
¼ teaspoon sea salt

SAUCE

100g (3½oz) walnuts, soaked
1 teaspoon mushroom stock (broth)
2 teaspoons tamari soy sauce

TOPPING

extra virgin olive oil, for drizzling
a sprinkle of broken walnuts
a sprinkle of fresh oregano
sea salt and freshly ground black
  pepper, to taste

METHOD

MAIN VEG

Preheat the oven to 200°C (400°F)/gas mark 6. Slice the bottom off the squash and slice it again horizontally in the middle (where the curve ends and the seeds starts). Reserve the top half for another recipe (see page 184). Scoop out all the seeds and wash the inside well. You will be left with a big ring.

Place the squash on a baking tray (sheet) lined with baking paper, drizzle with oil, sprinkle with salt and place the oregano in the middle of the ring. Bake for 45–50 minutes until completely tender. Remove from the oven and discard the burned oregano.

PROTEIN/CARB

Heat the olive oil in a pan over a medium heat and sauté the shallot until transparent but not burned. Add the beans and salt and stir together until combined and nice and warm.

SAUCE

Boil 150ml (5¼fl oz) in a saucepan. Add the mushroom stock (broth) and stir until fully dissolved. Remove from the heat and add the walnuts and tamari soy sauce. Blend until smooth.

ASSEMBLING

Spoon the sauce onto a plate and arrange the squash on top. Fill the squash up with the black beans, drizzle with extra virgin olive oil and scatter over the toppings.

CROWN SQUASH WITH ROASTED POTATOES & TOMATO SAUCE

INGREDIENTS

PROTEIN/CARB

1 large potato, peeled and
   thinly sliced
2 teaspoons olive oil
a handful of fresh rosemary,
   finely chopped
sea salt, to taste

MAIN VEG

½ small crown squash, scrubbed to
   remove the wax
2 tablespoons vegetable oil
1 teaspoon brown sugar
1 teaspoon sea salt

SAUCE

1 tablespoon olive oil
½ red onion, finely chopped
2 tablespoons grated carrot
1 garlic clove, minced
200g (7oz) chopped tomatoes
1 tablespoon capers
1 teaspoon chilli flakes
1 teaspoon brown sugar
¼ teaspoon salt

TOPPING

a sprinkle of fresh basil leaves
a sprinkle of coarsely ground
   pumpkin seeds

METHOD

PROTEIN/CARB

Preheat the oven to 200°C (400°F)/gas mark 6. Place the potato slices on a baking tray (sheet) lined with baking paper, drizzle with olive oil and sprinkle with rosemary. Bake for 25–30 minutes until golden and crunchy around the edges. Season with salt to taste.

MAIN VEG

Slice the squash in half lengthwise, scoop out all the seeds and wash the insides well. Place the squash on a baking tray (sheet) lined with baking paper, hollow-side up, drizzle with oil, sprinkle with sugar and salt and bake for 25–35 minutes until tender.

SAUCE

Heat the olive oil in a pan over a medium heat and sauté the onion with the carrot and garlic for about 5 minutes, being careful not to let it burn. Add the tomato, capers, chilli, sugar and salt, then cover with a lid and simmer for 20 minutes.

ASSEMBLING

Arrange the roasted potato on a plate, top with the squash, hollow-side up, and fill with the tomato sauce. Scatter over the toppings.

ALTERNATIVE TIP
If you want a swap the
potatoes for another carb,
how about beans, corn or
a chickpea (garbanzo bean)
pancake (page 83)?

ALTERNATIVE TIP
If you want a more classic
Korean- inspired carb, opt
for white rice instead of the
quinoa, but also lentils or
buckwheat will do the job
very well.

ROASTED SQUASH WITH QUINOA & HOT BULGOGI SAUCE

INGREDIENTS

PROTEIN/CARB
50g (2oz) quinoa
1 tablespoon olive oil
a pinch of sea salt

MAIN VEG
1/2 large butternut squash, scrubbed
  to remove the wax
2 tablespoons vegetable oil
1 teaspoon salt

SAUCE
1/2 pear, cored
1/2 garlic clove, chopped
1 tablespoon miso paste
1 tablespoon grated fresh ginger
1 teaspoon toasted sesame oil
juice of 1/2 grapefruit
1/2 fresh small red chilli, deseeded

TOPPING
a sprinkle of toasted sesame seeds
1 spring onion (scallion),
  finely chopped

METHOD

PROTEIN/CARB
Place the quinoa in a sieve and rinse under cold running water to remove all the soapy coating and get rid of any bitter flavour. Transfer the quinoa to a saucepan, cover with 100ml (3½fl oz) water and bring to the boil. Reduce the heat, cover with a lid and simmer for 15–20 minutes. Stir in the oil and season with salt.

MAIN VEG
Preheat the oven to 200°C (400°F)/gas mark 6. Slice the squash in half lengthwise, scoop out all the seeds and wash the insides. Using a sharp knife, score the squash diagonally all over (see image).

Place the squash on a baking tray (sheet) lined with baking paper, hollow-side up, drizzle with oil, sprinkle with salt and bake for 25–35 minutes until tender.

SAUCE
Place all the ingredients in a blender and blend until smooth.

ASSEMBLING
Spoon the quinoa onto a plate and drizzle over the sauce. Arrange the squash on top and scatter over the toppings.

ROASTED SQUASH, TOASTED PUMPKIN SEEDS & MUSHROOM BÉCHAMEL

INGREDIENTS

PROTEIN/CARB

60g (2½oz) pumpkin seeds
1 tablespoon extra virgin olive oil
¼ teaspoon sea salt

MAIN VEG

1 large butternut squash,
  scrubbed to remove the wax
2 tablespoons extra virgin olive oil
1 teaspoon sea salt
a sprig of fresh rosemary

SAUCE

3 tablespoons olive oil
1 garlic clove, finely chopped
2 brown mushrooms,
  finely chopped
100ml (3½fl oz) oat (soya or rice) milk
2 tablespoons gluten-free flour of
  your choice (oat, buckwheat or rice)
¼ teaspoon salt

TOPPING

a sprinkle of pumpkin seeds
a sprinkle of fresh oregano
a drizzle of balsamic glaze

METHOD

PROTEIN/CARB

Preheat the oven to 160°C (325°F)/gas mark 3. Spread the pumpkin seeds out over a baking tray (sheet) lined with a baking paper, drizzle with oil and sprinkle with salt. Bake for 15 minutes.

MAIN VEG

Slice the bottom off the squash and slice it again horizontally in the middle (where the curve ends and the seeds starts). Reserve the bottom half for another recipe (see page 179) and cut the top half into long slices, as thin as you can.

Increase the oven to 200°C (400°F)/gas mark 6. Arrange the squash slices on a baking tray (sheet) lined with baking paper, drizzle with oil, sprinkle with salt and lay the rosemary on top. Bake for 25–35 minutes until completely tender. Remove from the oven and discard the burned rosemary.

SAUCE

Heat the oil in a pan over a medium heat and sauté the garlic for about 5 minutes, being careful not to let it burn, then add the mushrooms and sauté for a further 10 minutes. Add the milk and simmer for 5 minutes, then sift in the flour and stir over a low heat until slightly thickened but completely smooth. If the sauce is too thick, add a little more milk. If you want a very creamy sauce, place in a blender and blend until smooth. Season to taste.

ASSEMBLING

Stack the roasted squash slices in layers, separating each one with a tablespoon of sauce and some of the pumpkin seeds. Use the rest of the seeds as a topping, along with a sprinkle of oregano and balsamic glaze.

ALTERNATIVE TIP

If you want a more classic
carb, instead of the pumpkin
seeds you can use lentils,
quinoa or buckwheat and
keep the seeds just for
the topping.

ALTERNATIVE TIP -
If you are not keen on
chimichurri, you can use
tahini (page 168) or avocado
sauce (page 175).

CROWN SQUASH WITH BLACK LENTILS & CHIMICHURRI

INGREDIENTS

PROTEIN/CARB

60g (2½oz) black lentils
1 tablespoon olive oil
½ teaspoon sea salt

MAIN VEG

½ small crown squash, scrubbed to
  remove the wax
2 tablespoons vegetable oil
1 teaspoon brown sugar
1 teaspoon salt

SAUCE

125ml (4fl oz) extra virgin olive oil
juice of ½ lemon
2 garlic cloves
30g (1oz) fresh flat-leaf parsley,
  finely chopped
1 tablespoon finely chopped fresh
  mint
½ teaspoon salt
a sprinkle of black pepper

TOPPING

a sprinkle of almond flakes
a sprinkle of chilli flakes

METHOD

PROTEIN/CARB

Rinse the lentils with fresh water before cooking. Transfer to a pan, together with 180ml (6¼fl oz) water and bring to the boil, then reduce the heat, cover tightly and simmer for 15–20 minutes until tender. Stir through the oil and salt after cooking.

MAIN VEG

Preheat the oven to 200°C (400°F)/gas mark 6. Slice the squash in half lengthwise, scoop out all the seeds and wash the insides well. Place the squash on a baking tray (sheet) lined with baking paper, hollow-side up, drizzle with oil, sprinkle with sugar and salt and bake for 25–35 minutes until tender.

SAUCE

Place all the ingredients in a blender and blend until smooth.

ASSEMBLING

Spoon half the sauce onto a plate and lay the squash on top, hollow-side up. Fill with the lentils, drizzle over the remaining sauce and finish with a scatter of toppings.

KATZU CELERIAC (CELERY ROOT) WITH BASMATI RICE & CURRY SAUCE

INGREDIENTS

PROTEIN/CARB
50g (2oz) cooked basmati rice

MAIN VEG
1 slice of celeriac
   (celery root), 2.5cm-/1in-thick
4 tablespoons rapeseed oil or
   vegetable oil
1 tablespoon cornflour
50g (2oz) gluten-free breadcrumbs
sea salt and freshly ground black
   pepper, to taste

SAUCE
1 teaspoon rapeseed oil or vegetable
   oil
1 onion, chopped
1 carrot, chopped
1 garlic clove, crushed
a thumb-sized piece of fresh ginger,
   peeled and grated
1 tablespoon curry powder
½ teaspoon ground turmeric
100ml (3½fl oz) coconut milk
2 teaspoons maple syrup

TOPPING
a sprinkle of sesame seeds
a handful of fresh flat-leaf
   parsley leaves

METHOD

MAIN VEG
Preheat the oven to 200°C (400°F)/gas mark 6. Place the celeriac steak on a baking tray (sheet) lined with baking paper, drizzle with 1 tablespoon of oil and bake in the oven for 20–30 minutes until tender.

In a wide, shallow bowl, mix the cornflour with 4 tablespoons water and some seasoning. In a second bowl, place the breadcrumbs. Dip the roasted celeriac first into the flour mixture and then into the breadcrumbs, turning until well coated. Heat the remaining oil in a frying pan over a medium–high heat and cook the celeriac for 4–5 minutes on each side until golden.

SAUCE
Heat the oil in a deep pan over a medium heat and sauté the onion and carrot for about 8 minutes, until starting to caramelize. Add the garlic and ginger and sizzle for 30 seconds, then stir in the curry powder and turmeric. Stir through the coconut milk, maple syrup and 3½ tablespoons water. Season, cover and simmer over a low heat for 20 minutes. Check that the onions and carrots in the sauce are soft, then transfer to a blender and blitz until smooth.

ASSEMBLING
Spoon the sauce onto a plate and top with the rice and celeriac steak, sliced into thin strips. Scatter over the parsley and sesame seeds.

ALTERNATIVE TIP
Swap the curry sauce for a
hot Korean-style one on
page 204.

ALTERNATIVE TIP
Many carbs work very well in
this recipe, like bread chunks,
buckwheat chunks or lentils.

TRUFFLE CELERIAC (CELERY ROOT) STEAK WITH BLACK BEANS & CASHEW CREAM

INGREDIENTS

PROTEIN/CARB
2 tablespoons olive oil
1 small onion, finely chopped
½ teaspoon of brown sugar
120g (4½oz) cooked black beans
sea salt, to taste

MAIN VEG
2 slices of celeriac (celery root),
 2.5cm-/1in-thick
2 tablespoons rapeseed oil or vegetable oil

SAUCE
100g (3½oz) cashew nuts, soaked
1 tablespoon nutritional yeast
2 teaspoons tamari soy sauce

TOPPING
a generous sprinkle of coarse black pepper
a sprinkle of chia seeds
a sprinkle of fresh oregano
a drizzle of truffle oil

METHOD

PROTEIN/CARB
Heat the olive oil in a pan over a medium heat and sauté the onion until transparent but not burned. Stir through sugar, salt and finally the black beans, then take off the heat and set aside, covered, for the beans to warm through.

MAIN VEG
Preheat the oven to 200°C (400°F)/gas mark 6. Place the celeriac steak on a baking tray (sheet) lined with baking paper, drizzle with 1 tablespoon of oil (reserving the rest for later) and bake in the oven for 20–30 minutes until softer and golden but still quite firm. Heat 1 tablespoon oil in a frying pan and cook the celeriac for 4–5 minutes on each side until golden and tender.

SAUCE
Place all the ingredients in a blender with 100ml (3½fl oz) water and blend until smooth.

ASSEMBLING
Spoon the beans onto a plate along with the sauce. Lay the celeriac steaks on top and scatter over the toppings.

CELERIAC (CELERY ROOT) STEAK WITH BLACK RICE & BULGOGI SAUCE

INGREDIENTS

PROTEIN/CARB
60g (2½oz) black rice

MAIN VEG
1–2 slices of celeriac (celery root),
 2.5cm-/1in-thick,
 depending on diameter
2 tablespoon rapeseed oil or
 vegetable oil
sea salt and freshly ground
 black pepper, to taste

SAUCE
½ pear, cored
1 garlic clove, chopped
1 tablespoon miso paste
1 tablespoon grated fresh ginger
1 teaspoon toasted sesame oil
juice of ½ grapefruit

TOPPING
a sprinkle of toasted sesame seeds
1 spring onion (scallion), finely chopped
½ red chilli pepper, finely chopped

METHOD

PROTEIN/CARB
Place the rice in a pan in a saucepan, cover with 180ml (6¼fl oz) water. Bring to the boil over a medium heat, then reduce to a simmer, cover and cook for around 45 minutes or until you have your preferred texture (black rice will always be pretty chewy). Top up with more water if needed.

MAIN VEG
Preheat the oven to 200°C (400°F)/gas mark 6. Place the celeriac steak on a baking tray (sheet) lined with baking paper, drizzle with 1 tablespoon of oil (reserving the rest for later) and bake in the oven for 20–30 minutes until softer and golden but still quite firm. Heat 1 tablespoon oil in a frying pan and cook the celeriac for 4–5 minutes on each side until golden.

SAUCE
Place all the ingredients in a blender and blend until smooth.

ASSEMBLING
Spoon the sauce onto a plate and arrange the rice and celeriac on top. Scatter over the sesame seeds, spring onion and chilli.

ALTERNATIVE TIP
If you want you, can swap the bulgogi sauce for the Indian-inspired curry sauce on page 28 or the hot Mexican-inspired one on page 31.

ALTERNATIVE TIP
If you want, you can swap
the teriyaki sauce for the
tomato one on page 56, or
the mustard one on page 152.

ROASTED SWEDE (RUTABAGA) WITH WHITE RICE & TERIYAKI SAUCE

INGREDIENTS

PROTEIN/CARB
60g (2½oz) white short rice
1 tablespoon olive oil
a pinch of sea salt

MAIN VEG
1–2 slices of swede (rutabaga)
  2.5cm-/1in-thick,
  depending on diameter
1 tablespoon oil

SAUCE
2 tablespoons soy sauce
1 tablespoon toasted sesame oil
2 tablespoons fresh orange juice
1 teaspoon brown sugar
2 garlic cloves, minced
1 teaspoon fresh grated ginger
1 tablespoon vegetable oil

TOPPING
a sprinkle of toasted sesame seeds
1 spring onion (scallion), finely chopped

METHOD

PROTEIN/CARB
Place the rice in a saucepan with 180ml (6¼fl oz) water, stir through the oil and salt and bring to the boil. Reduce the heat, cover with a lid and simmer for 20 minutes.

MAIN VEG
First make the sauce (see below). Preheat the oven to 200°C (400°F)/gas mark 6. Place the swede steak on a baking tray (sheet) lined with baking paper, drizzle with 1 tablespoon of oil and bake in the oven for 20–30 minutes until soft and golden but still quite firm. Heat 2 tablespoons of the sauce in a frying pan and cook the swede for 1–2 minutes on each side until golden and tender.

SAUCE
Place all the marinade ingredients in a blender and blend until completely smooth.

ASSEMBLING
Spoon the rice onto a plate along with the sauce. Lay the swede on top and scatter over the toppings.

ROASTED SWEDE (RUTABAGA), SAFFRON POLENTA & MUSHROOM GRAVY

INGREDIENTS

PROTEIN/CARB
100g (3¹/₂oz) quick polenta
¹/₂ teaspoon saffron
1 tablespoon vegan butter or margarine
sea salt and freshly ground black
  pepper, to taste

MAIN VEG
1–2 slices of swede (rutabaga)
  (2.5cm-/1in-thick),
  depending on diameter
3 tablespoon extra virgin olive oil
4 sage leaves

SAUCE
2 tablespoons olive oil
2 brown mushrooms, finely chopped
1 garlic clove, minced
a handful of fresh sage leaves
¹/₄ teaspoon salt
100ml (3¹/₂fl oz) oat cream
1 tablespoon gluten-free flour of your
  choice (oat, buckwheat or rice)

TOPPING
a drizzle of extra virgin olive oil
a sprinkle of saffron
sea salt and freshly ground black
  pepper, to taste

METHOD

PROTEIN/CARB
Place 400ml (1³/₄ cups) water in a pan, add the saffron and bring to boil over a medium heat. Slowly pour in the polenta and stir for about 3 minutes, until the mixture thickens. Take off the heat, stir through the vegan butter and season to taste.

MAIN VEG
Preheat the oven to 200°C (400°F)/gas mark 6. Place the swede steak on a baking tray (sheet) lined with baking paper, drizzle with 1 tablespoon oil and bake in the oven for 20–30 minutes until softer and golden but still quite firm.

Heat 2 tablespoons oil in a frying pan and fry the sage leaves until crisp, then remove from the pan and fry the swede steak in the sage oil for 1–2 minutes on each side until golden and tender. Reserve the sage for the topping.

SAUCE
Heat the olive oil in a pan over a medium heat and sauté the mushroom and garlic for 5–10 minutes, being careful not to let it burn. Stir through the salt, sage and oat cream, cover with a lid and simmer for 5 minutes. Strain the contents of the pan through a colander, reserving only the liquid. Return the liquid to the pan, sift in the flour and stir gently over a low heat until slightly thickened and completely smooth.

ASSEMBLING
Spoon the polenta onto a plate, followed by the sauce. Lay the swede steak on top and scatter over the toppings.

ALTERNATIVE TIP
Many carbs work very well
in this recipe, like roasted
potatoes, buckwheat chunks
or lentils.

ALTERNATIVE TIP
Other grains can work very well in this recipe like quinoa, oats or even buckwheat.

KOHLRABI STEAK WITH MUSHROOM & PINK PEPPER RISOTTO

INGREDIENTS

PROTEIN/CARB

2 tablespoons extra virgin olive oil

½ shallot, finely chopped

1 garlic clove, finely chopped

2 brown mushrooms, finely chopped

1 teaspoon vegetable bouillon powder

60g (2½oz) risotto rice

½ teaspoon salt

1 tablespoon vegan butter

sea salt and freshly ground black
   pepper, to taste

MAIN VEG

½ kohlrabi, peeled, topped and tailed

a sprig of fresh rosemary

2 tablespoons extra virgin olive oil
   plus extra, for drizzling

1 tablespoon maple syrup or
   brown sugar

2 tablespoons mushroom broth (or
   2 tablespoons plant-based milk mixed
   with ½ teaspoon mushroom
   stock/broth)

1 tablespoon pink peppercorns

1 teaspoon sea salt,
   plus extra for sprinkling

TOPPINGS

   a drizzle of extra virgin olive oil

   1 teaspoon crumbled toasted hazelnuts

   1 teaspoon fresh dill

METHOD

PROTEIN/CARB/SAUCE

Heat the oil in a pan over a medium heat and gently fry the shallot and garlic for 10–15 minutes until softened, then add the mushrooms and fry gently for a further 10–15 minutes.

Place the vegetable bouillon powder in a jug, pour over 120ml (3¾fl oz) boiling water and stir to dissolve. Add the rice to the pan and turn up the heat – the rice will now begin to lightly fry, so keep stirring (after a minute it will look slightly translucent). Add the vegetable stock (broth) a ladle at a time and keep stirring. Turn the heat down to a simmer, add the salt and keep adding the stock (broth), slowly slowly, stirring often, for around 15 minutes is tender and creamy. Take off the heat, stir in the butter and season to taste with salt and pepper.

MAIN VEG

Slice the kohlrabi in half horizontally to make two steaks and deeply score the surface of each one. Place the remaining ingredients in a resealable bag, add the kohlrabi, ensuring it is thoroughly coated, then set aside to marinate for at least 15–20 minutes (or ideally overnight).

Preheat the oven to 200°C (400°F)/gas mark 6. Remove the kohlrabi from the marinade and place on a baking tray (sheet) lined with baking paper, drizzle with oil, sprinkle with salt and place in the oven for 50 minutes. Remove from the oven, pour the marinade on top and bake for a further 15–20 minutes until completely tender. Reserve the roasted pink peppercorns for later as a topping.

ASSEMBLING

Spoon the risotto onto a plate and arrange the kohlrabi on top. Drizzle with extra virgin olive oil, season and scatter over the nuts, dill and reserved peppercorns.

GOCHUJANG TURNIP WITH QUINOA & SRIRACHA MAYO

INGREDIENTS

MAIN VEG

1 large turnip, topped and tailed

2 garlic cloves, crushed

2.5cm- (1in-) piece of fresh ginger, peeled and finely chopped

1 tablespoon tamari soy sauce

1 tablespoon gochujang (Korean hot pepper paste) or harissa paste

1 tablespoon mirin (sweet Japanese rice wine) or orange juice

1 teaspoon rice syrup or maple syrup

2 tablespoons vegetable oil

PROTEIN/CARB

50g (2oz) quinoa

1 tablespoon olive oil

a pinch of sea salt

SAUCE

1 tablespoon sriracha sauce

3 tablespoons vegan mayo

TOPPING

1 teaspoon toasted sesame seeds

1 spring onion (scallion), finely chopped

METHOD

MAIN VEG

Slice the turnip in half horizontally so that you make two steaks that are each 5cm- (2in-) thick (see image). Place the remaining ingredients in a resealable bag and add the turnip, ensuring it is thoroughly coated, then set aside to marinate for at least 15–20 minutes (or ideally overnight).

Preheat the oven to 200°C (400°F)/gas mark 6. Remove the turnip from the marinade and place on a baking tray (sheet) lined with baking paper, drizzle with oil, sprinkle with salt and place in the oven for 30 minutes. Remove from the oven, pour the marinade on top and bake for a further 15–20 minutes until completely tender.

PROTEIN/CARB

Place the quinoa in a sieve and rinse under cold running water to remove all the soapy coating and get rid of any bitter flavour. Transfer the quinoa to a saucepan, cover with 100ml (3½fl oz) water, stir through the oil and salt and bring to the boil. Reduce the heat, cover with a lid and simmer for 15–20 minutes.

SAUCE

In a bowl, mix mayo and sriracha sauce until well combined.

ASSEMBLING

Spoon the sauce onto a plate, followed by the quinoa. Place the turnip steaks on top and scatter over sesame seeds and spring onion.

WATCH THE ONLINE RECIPE

ALTERNATIVE TIP

Many other carbs can work very well in this recipe, like beans, buckwheat or chickpeas (garbanzo beans).

ALTERNATIVE TIP
Many other carbs can work
very well in this recipe, like
beans, buckwheat, quinoa or
chickpeas (garbanzo beans).

ROASTED TURNIP WITH WHITE RICE & CHIMICHURRI SAUCE

INGREDIENTS

MAIN VEG

2 garlic cloves, crushed

1 tablespoon cider vinegar

2 tablespoons vegetable oil

1 teaspoon sea salt

1 teaspoon coarse black pepper

1 large turnip or 2 smaller ones, topped and tailed

PROTEIN/CARB

50g (1¾oz) white rice

1 tablespoon olive oil

a pinch sea salt

SAUCE

30g (1oz) fresh flat-leaf parsley, finely chopped

2 garlic cloves

1 tablespoon finely chopped fresh mint

juice of ½ lemon

125ml (4fl oz) extra virgin olive oil

½ teaspoon salt

a sprinkle of black pepper

TOPPINGS

1 teaspoon toasted sunflower seeds

a sprig of fresh flat-leaf parsley, finely chopped

METHOD

MAIN VEG

Place the garlic, vinegar, oil, salt and pepper in a resealable bag and add the turnip, ensuring it is thoroughly coated, then set aside to marinate for at least 15–20 minutes (or ideally overnight).

Preheat the oven to 200°C (400°F)/gas mark 6. Remove the turnip from the marinade and place on a baking tray (sheet) lined with baking paper, drizzle with oil, sprinkle with salt and place in the oven for 40 minutes. Remove from the oven, pour the marinade on top and bake for a further 15 minutes until tender.

PROTEIN/CARB

Place in a saucepan, cover with 100ml (3½fl oz) water, stir through the oil and salt and bring to the boil. Reduce the heat, cover with a lid and simmer for 15–20 minutes.

SAUCE

Place all the ingredients in a blender and blend until smooth.

ASSEMBLING

Spoon the rice onto a plate and drizzle over the sauce. Arrange the turnip on top, then scatter over the sunflower seeds and fresh parsley.

ROASTED TURNIP WITH BORLOTTI BEANS & LEMON SAUCE

INGREDIENTS

MARINADE/SAUCE
2 tablespoons lemon juice
3 tablespoons extra virgin olive oil
1 tablespoon maple syrup or brown sugar
a handful of fresh thyme
1 teaspoon sea salt

PROTEIN/CARB
120g (4¼oz) cooked borlotti beans

MAIN VEG
1 large turnip, topped and tailed
a sprinkle of salt
2 tablespoons olive oil

TOPPINGS
1 teaspoon hulled hemp seeds
1 teaspoon fresh lemon thyme
1 teaspoon grated lemon zest

METHOD

MARINADE/SAUCE
Place all the ingredients in a blender and blend until smooth, then transfer the sauce to a pan and warm through over a low heat. Add the beans, stirring to combine, and cook for 2–3 minutes.

MAIN VEG
Preheat the oven to 200°C (400°F)/gas mark 6. Slice the turnip into three or four discs, 2.5cm-/(1in-) thick. Arrange on a baking tray (sheet) lined with baking paper, drizzle with oil, sprinkle with salt and bake in the oven for 15–20 minutes until softer and golden, but still quite firm. Remove from the oven, place two-thirds of the marinade on top of the veg. Bake for another 15–20 minutes depending on the size of the veg till soft enough to pierce it through.

PROTEIN/CARB
Heat up a pan on medium heat and place the beans and a third of the sauce and stir until warm.

ASSEMBLING
Spoon the beans onto a plate and lay the turnip on top. Scatter with the hemp seeds, lemon thyme and lemon zest.

ALTERNATIVE TIP
Many other carbs can work
very well in this recipe, like
buckwheat, quinoa or even
chickpeas (garbanzo beans).

ALTERNATIVE TIP
This recipe works with other
carbs, like aduki or mung
beans, and red lentils too.

SWEET POTATO WITH YELLOW PEA DAHL & COCONUT YOGURT

INGREDIENTS

PROTEIN/CARB
60g (2½oz) yellow split peas
200ml (7fl oz) coconut milk
1 teaspoon ground cinnamon
1 teaspoon ground turmeric
1 teaspoon ground ginger
1 tablespoon olive oil
½ teaspoon cumin seeds
½ small onion, finely chopped
2.5cm- (1in-) piece of fresh ginger,
  peeled and finely chopped
1 garlic clove, finely chopped
½ teaspoon ground coriander (cilantro)
½ teaspoon salt
1 small tomato, chopped
1 teaspoon lemon juice
a bunch of fresh coriander (cilantro),
  finely chopped

MAIN VEG
1 large sweet potato, scrubbed
1 tablespoon olive oil
½ teaspoon sea salt

SAUCE
2 tablespoons vegan yogurt (coconut)

TOPPINGS
1 teaspoon toasted coconut flakes
a sprinkle of fresh coriander leaves
  (cilantro)
a sprinkle of smoked paprika

METHOD

PROTEIN/CARB
Rinse the split peas with fresh water before cooking to remove any dust or debris. Transfer to a pan, together with the milk and cinnamon stick and stir through the turmeric and ginger. Bring to the boil, then reduce the heat, cover and allow to simmer for 30–45 minutes until tender and most of the liquid has been absorbed.

Meanwhile, heat the oil in a frying pan over a medium heat and fry the cumin seeds for 30 seconds, then add the onion and ginger and fry until the onion is soft. Add the garlic, ground coriander (cilantro) and salt and fry for a further 2 minutes. Add the tomato, plus 2 tablespoons water and bring to a gentle simmer, cooking for 20–30 minutes. When cooked, stir the spice mix into the split peas. Squeeze in the lemon juice and top with fresh coriander (cilantro).

MAIN VEG
Preheat the oven to 200°C (400°F)/gas mark 6. Slice the sweet potato thinly (see pic), then arrange the discs on a baking tray (sheet) lined with baking paper. Drizzle with oil, sprinkle with salt and bake for 20–30 minutes until golden.

ASSEMBLING
Spoon the dahl onto a plate and top with the yogurt. Arrange the sweet potato on top and scatter over the coconut flakes, coriander (cilantro) and smoked paprika.

SWEET POTATO WITH COUSCOUS & TOMATO SAUCE

INGREDIENTS

PROTEIN/CARB

60g (2½oz) gluten-free couscous (corn or
  chickpea – garbanzo bean – are great)
1 tablespoon olive oil
½ teaspoon salt

MAIN VEG

½ sweet potato, scrubbed
2 tablespoons extra virgin olive oil
1 teaspoon sea salt
a sprig of fresh oregano

SAUCE

2 tablespoons olive oil
½ shallot, finely chopped
1 garlic clove, finely chopped
200g (7oz) chopped tomatoes
1 teaspoon brown sugar
¼ teaspoon salt

TOPPING

a drizzle of extra virgin olive oil
1 teaspoon capers
1 teaspoon fresh oregano leaves
a sprinkle of chilli flakes
sea salt and freshly ground black
  pepper, to taste

METHOD

PROTEIN/CARB

In a heatproof bowl, place the couscous and stir through the oil and salt. Pour over 120ml (3¾fl oz) boiling water, cover with a towel or a lid and leave it for a couple of minutes. then uncover, mix well and season to taste.

MAIN VEG

Preheat the oven to 200°C (400°F)/gas mark 6. Cut the sweet potato in half lengthwise (this will make two steaks, see image) and place on a baking tray (sheet) lined with baking paper. Drizzle with oil, sprinkle with salt and oregano and bake in the oven for 30–45 minutes until tender.

SAUCE

Heat the olive oil in a pan over a medium heat and sauté the shallot and garlic until transparent but not burned. Add the tomatoes, sugar and salt, then cover with a lid and simmer for 20 minutes.

ASSEMBLING

Spoon the sauce onto a plate, followed by the couscous, then arrange the baked sweet potato on top, drizzle with oil, season and scatter over all the remaining toppings.

ALTERNATIVE TIP
Many other carbs can work
very well with this recipe,
like buckwheat or chickpeas
(garbanzo beans).

ALTERNATIVE TIP
Many other carbs can work
very well with this recipe,
like buckwheat, chickpeas
(garbanzo beans).

BAKED SWEET POTATO WITH BUCKWHEAT & CHIMICHURRI SAUCE

INGREDIENTS

PROTEIN/CARB

60g (2½oz) buckwheat
1 tablespoon olive oil
a pinch of sea salt

MAIN VEG

½ sweet potato, scrubbed
2 tablespoons extra virgin olive oil
1 teaspoon sea salt
a sprig of fresh oregano

SAUCE

30g (1oz) fresh flat-leaf parsley, finely
  chopped
2 garlic cloves
1 tablespoon finely chopped fresh
  mint
juice of ½ lemon
125ml (4fl oz) extra virgin olive oil
½ teaspoon sea salt
a sprinkle of black pepper

TOPPING

a drizzle of extra virgin olive oil
a handful of fresh pomegranate
  seeds
sea salt and freshly ground black
  pepper, to taste

METHOD

PROTEIN/CARB

Place the buckwheat in a deep pan, cover with 120ml (3¾fl oz) water and bring to the boil. Reduce to a simmer, cover and cook until the water has evaporated completely. Strain the buckwheat through a colander and rinse under hot water to remove the starchy and foxy bits. Set aside to drain, then when it's dry, transfer to a bowl and stir through the oil and sea salt to taste.

MAIN VEG

Preheat the oven to 200°C (400°F)/gas mark 6. Cut the sweet potato in half lengthwise, to make two steaks, score the cut side in a criss-cross fashion, and place on a baking tray (sheet) lined with baking paper. Drizzle with oil, sprinkle with salt and oregano and bake in the oven for 30–45 minutes until tender.

SAUCE

Place all the ingredients in a blender and blend until smooth.

ASSEMBLING

Spoon the sauce onto a plate, followed by the buckwheat. Arrange the baked sweet potato on top and finish with the toppings.

SWEET POTATO WITH BUCKWHEAT PANCAKES & TAHINI CREAM

INGREDIENTS

PROTEIN/CARB
60g (2½oz) buckwheat flour
1 teaspoon activated charcoal
2 tablespoons extra virgin olive oil
1 teaspoon salt
a handful of fresh tarragon leaves

MAIN VEG
1 small sweet potato, scrubbed
2 tablespoons extra virgin olive oil
1 teaspoon sea salt

SAUCE
1 tablespoon tahini
3½ tablespoons plant-based milk
  (rice or oat work best)
1 teaspoon lemon juice
1 teaspoon English mustard
½ teaspoon date or maple syrup
½ teaspoon sea salt

TOPPING
1 tablespoon extra virgin olive oil,
  plus extra for drizzling
2 brown mushrooms, thinly sliced
1 teaspoon finely chopped fresh
  flat-leaf parsley
1 teaspoon broken cashew nuts
sea salt and freshly ground black
  pepper, to taste

METHOD

PROTEIN/CARB
Tip the flour and charcoal in a bowl or blender. Slowly pour in 1 tablespoon of extra virgin olive oil (reserving the rest for later) and 120ml (3¾fl oz) water, beating with a whisk until you have a smooth, light batter (no lumps). Add the salt and tarragon and mix well. Heat the remaining oil in a non-stick frying pan over a medium–high heat. Pour in the batter, tilting the pan a little to ensure a thin and even layer. When the sides are crispy enough and the top is bubbly, use a spatula to gently flip the pancake and cook the other side. Keep flipping until you reach your preferred texture. You can also make smaller pancakes (like in the picture) by pouring only half the mix into the pan at a time.

MAIN VEG
Preheat the oven to 200°C (400°F)/gas mark 6. Using a sharp knife, deeply score the sweet potato diagonally all along one side (see image). Place on a baking tray (sheet) lined with baking paper, drizzle with oil, sprinkle with salt and bake in the oven for 30–45 minutes until tender.

SAUCE
Place all the ingredients in a blender and blend until smooth. Check the consistency – add a little more tahini until creamy.

TOPPING
Heat the oil in a frying pan over a medium–high heat and sauté the mushrooms for 10–15 minutes.

ASSEMBLING
Spoon the sauce onto a plate and top with the pancakes and sweet potato. Season, drizzle with oil and scatter over the fried mushroom, parsley and cashews.

WATCH
THE ONLINE
RECIPE

ALTERNATIVE TIP
Many other sauces can work
very well with this recipe,
like yogurt (see page 136),
tahini (see page 168), or even
avocado (see page 164).

ALTERNATIVE TIP -
Many other sauces can work well with this recipe, such as yogurt (see page 136), bulgogi (see page 192), or even avocado (see page 175).

BAKED SWEET POTATO WITH BROWN LENTILS & HOT SAUCE

INGREDIENTS

PROTEIN/CARB
60g (2½oz) brown lentils

1 teaspoon smoked paprika

½ teaspoon cayenne pepper

2.5cm- (1in-) piece of fresh ginger, peeled and finely chopped

1 teaspoon coconut or brown sugar

1 tablespoon lemon juice

1 teaspoon vegetable bouillon powder

2 tablespoons olive oil

½ teaspoon sea salt

MAIN VEG
1 small sweet potato, scrubbed

2 tablespoons extra virgin olive oil

1 teaspoon sea salt

SAUCE
2 tablespoons sriracha sauce

TOPPING
1 teaspoon fresh coriander (cilantro) leaves

1 teaspoon sesame seeds

½ small fresh chilli pepper, deseeded and finely chopped

sea salt, to taste

METHOD

PROTEIN/CARB
Rinse the lentils with fresh water before cooking to remove any dust or debris. Transfer to a pan, together with 180ml (6¼fl oz) water. Stir through the spices, sugar, lemon juice and bouillon powder and bring to the boil, then reduce the heat, cover tightly and simmer for 15–20 minutes until tender. Stir through the oil and salt after cooking.

MAIN VEG
Preheat the oven to 200°C (400°F)/gas mark 6. Using a sharp knife, deeply score the sweet potato all along one side. Place on a baking tray (sheet) lined with baking paper, drizzle with oil, sprinkle with salt and bake in the oven for 30–45 minutes until tender.

ASSEMBLING
Spoon the lentils onto a plate, drizzle with the sriracha sauce and place the baked sweet potato on top. Season and scatter over all the toppings.

INDEX

Portobello mushroom with basil pesto & butter bean hummus 126–7
Portobello mushroom with black lentils & tomato sauce 150–1
Portobello mushroom with roasted corn & BBQ sauce 124–5
red onion, roasted potatoes & thyme & mushroom béchamel 138–9
roasted squash, toasted pumpkin seeds & mushroom béchamel 184–5
roasted swede, saffron polenta & mushroom gravy 196–7
smoked carrot 'bacon' with chickpea scramble & avocado 164–5
sweet potatoes with buckwheat pancakes & tahini cream 216–17

OATS
broccoli with oat groats & grapefruit sauce 96–7
mushroom steak with savoury saffron oat 'porridge' & dill 128–9
Portobello mushroom with roasted corn & BBQ sauce 124–5

ONIONS
caramelized white onion with kidney beans & red pepper sauce 144–5
red onion, roasted potatoes & thyme & mushroom béchamel 138–9
roasted red onion in an oregano & white wine cream 142–3
roasted red onion with buckwheat & coconut yoghurt 136–7
roasted white onion with red quinoa & lemon & mustard tahini cream 146–7
teriyaki red onion with avocado & chickpea pancakes & kimchi 140–1

PARSNIPS
caramelized parsnip with mushrooms & quinoa 172–3
roasted parsnip with aduki beans & smoked tomato sauce 176–7
tamari parsnip with jasmine rice & miso avocado sauce 174–5

PEARS
celeriac steak with black rice & bulgogi sauce 192–3
fried lettuce with black rice & bulgogi sauce 46–7
roasted squash with quinoa & hot bulgogi sauce 182–3

PEAS
baked cauliflower with yellow peas & tahini sauce 98–9
fried broccoli with pea cream & crispy, smoky potatoes 92–3
fried cauliflower with peas & cabbage slaw 102–3
maple-roasted carrot with steamed potatoes & pea cream 170–1
smoked roasted cabbage with green peas & oat cream 112–13
sweet potato with yellow pea dahl & coconut yoghurt 210–11

PEPPERS (BELL PEPPERS)
caramelized white onion with kidney beans & red pepper sauce 144–5
with hummus & red pepper sauce 58–9
roasted with fava beans & hummus 20–1
roasted with potato & curry sauce 28–9

stuffed with almond cream 18–19
stuffed with black chickpeas & coriander (cilantro) pesto 22–3
stuffed with chimichurri 26–7
stuffed with coconut yoghurt & smoked paprika lentils 24–5

PESTO
yellow (bell) pepper with black chickpeas (garbanzo beans) & coriander (cilantro) pesto 23
sliced tomato with basil pesto & almond 'ricotta' 39
lettuce with cannellini beans & coriander (cilantro) pesto 43
courgette (zucchini) with chickpea (garbanzo bean) scramble & pesto 51
aubergine (eggplant) with basil pesto & buckwheat 64
radicchio with sun-dried tomato pesto & black-eyed beans 72
roasted fennel with butter bean hummus & basil pesto 84
portobello mushroom with basil pesto & butter bean hummus 127
candy beetroot (beet) 'bresaola' with parsley pesto & chickpea (garbanzo bean) hummus 148

POLENTA
cauliflower, polenta & BBQ sauce 100–1

POTATOES
crown squash with roasted potatoes & tomato sauce 180–1
maple-roasted carrot with steamed potatoes & pea cream 170–1
mushroom, roasted potatoes & truffle oat cream 122–3
red onion, roasted potatoes & thyme & mushroom béchamel 138–9
roasted red (bell) pepper with potato & curry sauce 28–9
roasted red cabbage with potatoes & tomato sauce 110–11
stuffed tomato with mayo & steamed potato 34–5

QUINOA
baked cauliflower with quinoa & saffron béchamel 108–9
caramelized parsnip with mushrooms & quinoa 172–3
courgette, red quinoa, parsley & mint sauce 52–3
gochujang turnip with quinoa & Sriracha mayo 204–5
roasted carrots with smoked paprika & mustard yoghurt sauce 160–1
roasted squash with quinoa & hot bulgogi sauce 182–3
roasted white onion with red quinoa & lemon & mustard tahini cream 146–7

RADICCHIO
baked radicchio with red lentils & coconut 74–5
with chickpea pancakes & hot sauce 78–9
fried radicchio with almond 'ricotta' & balsamic glaze 76–7
smoked fennel with radicchio risotto & sour cream 86–7
with sun-dried tomato pesto & black-eyed beans 72–3

RICE

broccoli with a miso glaze & black rice 90–1

celeriac steak with black rice & bulgogi sauce 192–3

fried aubergine with black rice & tahini sauce 62–3

fried lettuce with black rice & bulgogi sauce 46–7

fried oyster mushrooms with jasmine rice & Sriracha sauce 132–3

katzu celeriac with basmati rice & curry sauce 188–9

kohlrabi steak with mushrooms & pink pepper risotto 202–3

peppers stuffed with almond cream 18–19

roasted butternut squash with black rice & walnut cream 178–9

roasted carrot with rice & sweet tamari sauce 162–3

roasted cauliflower with lemon & seaweed black rice 106–7

roasted Chinese cabbage with black rice & mustard tahini sauce 118–19

roasted fennel with black rice & mustard sauce 80–1

roasted turnip with white rice & chimichurri sauce 206–7

smoked fennel with radicchio risotto & sour cream 86–7

tamari parsnip with jasmine rice & miso avocado sauce 174–5

SEAWEED

roasted cauliflower with lemon & seaweed black rice 106–7

SQUASH

crown squash with black lentils & chimichurri 186–7

crown squash with roasted potatoes & tomato sauce 180–1

roasted butternut squash with black rice & walnut cream 178–9

roasted squash with quinoa & hot bulgogi sauce 182–3

roasted squash, toasted pumpkin seeds & mushroom béchamel 184–5

SWEDE

roasted swede, saffron polenta & mushroom gravy 196–7

roasted swede with white rice & teriyaki sauce 194–5

SWEET POTATO

baked sweet potato with brown lentils & hot sauce 218–19

baked sweet potato with buckwheat & chimichurri sauce 214–15

with buckwheat pancakes & tahini cream 216–17

sweet potato with couscous & tomato sauce 212–13

sweet potato with yellow pea dahl & coconut yoghurt 210–11

SWEETCORN

corn-stuffed tomato with caper yoghurt 36–7

Portobello mushroom with roasted corn & BBQ sauce 124–5

roasted cauliflower with corn & cinnamon tomato sauce 104–5

TAHINI

baked cauliflower with yellow peas & tahini sauce 98–9

BBQ carrot with tomato, beans & mushroom tahini sauce 168–9

courgette with black beans & tahini 54–5

fried aubergine with black rice & tahini sauce 62–3

fried oyster mushrooms with chickpea pancakes & tahini sauce 134–5

roasted white onion with red quinoa & lemon & mustard tahini cream 146–7

sweet potatoes with buckwheat pancakes & tahini cream 216–17

TOMATO SAUCE

aubergine 'parmigiana' with tomato sauce & almond 'ricotta' 66–7

courgette with tomato sauce & breadcrumbs 56–7

crown squash with roasted potatoes & tomato sauce 180–1

kohlrabi with borlotti beans & tomato sauce 200–1

Portobello mushroom with black lentils & tomato sauce 150–1

roasted broccoli with butter bean hummus & harissa tomato sauce 94–5

roasted cauliflower with corn & cinnamon tomato sauce 104–5

roasted parsnip with aduki beans & smoked tomato sauce 176–7

roasted red cabbage with potatoes & tomato sauce 110–11

sweet potato with couscous & tomato sauce 212–13

TOMATOES

corn-stuffed tomato with caper yoghurt 36–7

roasted fennel with chickpea pancake & tomato 82–3

sliced tomato with basil pesto & almond 'ricotta' 38–9

stuffed tomato with avocado cream & black beans 30–1

stuffed tomato with mayo & steamed potato 34–5

tomato steak on chickpea pancakes with hummus 32–3

truffle celeriac steak with black beans & cashew cream 190–1

TURNIP

gochujang turnip with quinoa & Sriracha mayo 204–5

roasted turnip with borlotti beans & lemon sauce 208–9

roasted turnip with white rice & chimichurri sauce 206–7

WALNUTS

roasted butternut squash with black rice & walnut cream 178–9

YOGHURT

aubergine with yoghurt & chickpeas 70–1

corn-stuffed tomato with caper yoghurt 36–7

roasted carrot with charcoal buckwheat pancakes & tarragon yoghurt 166–7

pointed cabbage shawarma with buckwheat & yoghurt sauce 116–17

roasted carrots with smoked paprika & mustard yoghurt sauce 160–1

roasted red onion with buckwheat & coconut yoghurt 136–7

stuffed red (bell) pepper with coconut yoghurt & smoked paprika lentils 24–5

sweet potato with yellow pea dahl & coconut yoghurt 210–11

yoghurt-coated baked broccoli with curried red lentils 88–9

ACKNOWLEDGEMENTS

I dedicate this book to my dad; I love him even when I don't show it enough.

I thank my son and my wife, the lights of my life, for constantly reminding me to be a better, kinder, more flexible and stronger person.

I thank my aunt and uncle, as they are always there, bringing rationality and love.

I thank Silvia Padiglioni, as without her, this book would not exist.

I thank my mom because she raised me with no fear of mistakes.

I thank my in-laws, as without them we would never have got through this crazy time.

I thank Corona for making me realize what's important in life.

I thank my agent Heather, who did an incredible job of listening to me and understanding my drive.

I thank my editor, Judith, for guiding me and waiting for me.

I thank Chiara (@chiararusso_photographs), for the beautiful photos on page 2 and page 6.

I thank Angela (@botanyshope5), for helping me with the plates.

I thank Antonio, for sharing with me two crazy years and teaching me so much about food.

I thank Carolina (@aenichi), for inspiring me to be a professional.

I thank Vassiliki and her mom, Toto, who taught me the Greek secret about tomato sauce and cinnamon!

I thank all the people who still believe in truth and values, and who stand for them.